Celebrating
CHILDREN'S CHOICES

25 YEARS OF CHILDREN'S FAVORITE BOOKS

Arden DeVries Post, Calvin College, Grand Rapids, Michigan, USA

With

Marilyn Scott, Ursuline College, Pepper Pike, Ohio, USA

Michelle Theberge, Aquidneck School, Middletown, Rhode Island, USA

INTERNATIONAL
**Reading
Association**®

800 Barksdale Road, PO Box 8139
Newark, Delaware 19714-8139, USA
www.reading.org

CO-AJW-140

Director of Publications   Joan M. Irwin
Editorial Director, Books and Special Projects   Matthew W. Baker
Special Projects Editor   Tori Mello Bachman
Permissions Editor   Janet S. Parrack
Associate Editor   Jeanine K. McGann
Production Editor   Shannon Benner
Editorial Assistant   Pamela McComas
Publications Coordinator   Beth Doughty
Production Department Manager   Iona Sauscermen
Art Director   Boni Nash
Supervisor, Electronic Publishing   Anette Schütz-Ruff
Electronic Publishing Specialist   Cheryl J. Strum
Electronic Publishing Assistant   John W. Cain

Project Editor   Janet S. Parrack

Library of Congress Cataloging in Publication Data
Post, Arden DeVries.
   Celebrating children's choices: 25 years of children's favorite books / Arden DeVries Post with Marilyn Scott, Michelle Theberge.
     p.   cm.
   Includes bibliographical references (p.) and index.
   ISBN 0-87207-276-2 (alk. paper)
   1. Best books—Children's literature.   2. Children's literature—Bibliography. 3. Children—Books and reading—Activity programs.   I. Scott, Marilyn. II. Theberge, Michelle.   III. Title.
Z1037 .P86   2000   00-044902
[PN1009.A1]
028.1'62—dc21

Contents

Acknowledgments

Appreciation is expressed to the following teachers who so generously shared their use of Children's Choices books in the classroom. They were part of a Teachers as Readers group that met monthly to discuss children's literature:

Kirsten Bolles
Grand Haven Christian School, Grand Haven, Michigan

Karen De Young
Moline Christian School, Moline, Michigan

JoAnn Van Vugt
Jenison Christian School, Jenison, Michigan

Rachel Westra
Grand Rapids Public Schools, Grand Rapids, Michigan

and

Erin Mulhall
St. Stephen Catholic School, East Grand Rapids, Michigan, who let a group of future teachers take over her class to inspire a love of history with books by Jean Fritz.

Appreciation is also expressed to the following future teachers at Calvin College, Grand Rapids, Michigan, who so creatively used Children's Choices books with children during their language arts course in which they planned integrated language arts lessons based around a theme using Jean Fritz books:

Rachelle Brink, Allendale, Michigan

Jeralyn DeVries, Modesto, California

Pennie Hale, Montrose, Colorado

Beth Holtgeerts, Holland, Michigan

Kelly Kenyon, Hemlock, Michigan

Kristin LeMahieu, Hudsonville, Michigan

Kevin Sills, Grand Rapids, Michigan

Meredith Woolman, Alpena, Michigan

Appreciation is expressed to the following future teachers at Calvin College, Grand Rapids, Michigan, for their creative planning of Spring Break activities, based on Children's Choices books, for urban children from the Grand Rapids Public Schools:

Marie Betten, Muskegon, Michigan

Liza Blackmer, Lakeview, Michigan

Erin Bos, Plano, Texas

Andrea Boverhof, Wellandport, Ontario, Canada

Kim Evenhouse, Villa Park, Illinois

Shari Faber, Grandville, Michigan

Jona Fimrite, St. Cloud, Minnesota

Amanda Helder, Grand Rapids, Michigan

Shelley Hoogstra, Wyoming, Michigan

Lynne Jeltema, Grand Rapids, Michigan

Lisa Kuiphof, Jenison, Michigan

Ivonne Melara, South Haven, Michigan

Sarah Riemersma, Grand Rapids, Michigan

Lisa Schuringa, Holland, Michigan

Amy TerMolen, Spring Lake, Michigan

Jennifer Van Essen, Muskegon, Michigan

Dena Velderman, Grand Rapids, Michigan

Louise Verhoef, St. Catharines, Ontario, Canada

Mary Zuiderveen-Oeverman, Grand Rapids, Michigan

and

Sarah Klein Vander Wall, Hawthorne, New Jersey, whose love of animals and children inspired a study of the Humane Societies.

We also gratefully acknowledge the creative endeavors of the following future teachers from Ursuline College in Pepper Pike, Ohio. Their use of Children's Choices books in their field placements was welcomed by their cooperating teachers and the elementary school children whom they taught. Some children were heard telling them, "Oh, please don't go, we love you so!" reminiscent of Max in *Where the Wild Things Are* by Maurice Sendak:

Bridget Freese

Nancy Lodge

Kathleen O'Neill

Aleigh Phillips

Gretchen Zeigler

Our East Coast contingent took its geographical location seriously and shared with us the school theme whales. They built the theme around *Katie K. Whale,* after falling in love with her. They went on to share other Children's Choices adventures they had with younger readers. We thank the following from Fall River, Massachusetts:

Kim Donovan

Lynn Silvia

Erin Sullivan

Brenda Wordell

And thank you to our faithful typists, editors, and commentators, without whom we could not have done this.

David Brasser, Grand Rapids, Michigan

Kellie De Witte, Hudsonville, Michigan

Bethany Haverkamp, Grand Rapids, Michigan

Teresa Macklin, Quincy, Michigan

Alicia Van Der Bill, Minneapolis, Minnesota

Credits

Chapter 3

From *Cows Can't Fly*. Jacket illustration copyright ©1998 by David Milgrim. Reprinted with permission of Penguin Putnam Inc.

From *Bunnicula: A Rabbit Tale of Mystery*. Jacket illustration copyright ©1979 by Alan Daniel. Reprinted with permission.

From *Cloudy with a Chance of Meatballs* by Judi Barrett. Jacket illustration copyright ©1978 by Ron Barrett. Reprinted with permission of Simon & Schuster/Atheneum.

From *Katie K. Whale* by Suzanne Tate. Jacket illustration copyright ©1995 by James Melvin. Reprinted with permission of Nags Head Art, Inc.

From *The Doorbell Rang*. Copyright ©1986 by Pat Hutchins. Reprinted with permission of HarperCollins.

From *The Magic School Bus Blows Its Top: A Book About Volcanoes* by Joanna Cole. Jacket illustration copyright ©1996 by Bruce Degen. Reprinted with permission of Scholastic Inc.

From *Miss Nelson Is Missing* by Harry Allard and James Marshall. Jacket illustration copyright ©1977 by James Marshall. Reprinted with permission of Houghton Mifflin Co. All rights reserved.

Chapter 4

From *American Tall Tales* by Mary Pope Osborne, wood engravings by Michael McCurdy. Cover illustration copyright ©1991 by Michael

Chapter 5

Afterword

Introduction

Through literature, students learn to explore possibilities and consider options for themselves and humankind. They come to find themselves, imagine others, value difference, and search for justice. They gain connectedness and seek vision. They become the literate thinkers we need to shape the decisions of tomorrow. (Langer, 1995, p. 1)

The importance of children's literature in instructional settings and in home environments is well-established. Coinciding with the use of children's literature by educators and parents has been the

virtual explosion...occurring in the book world: Thousands more outstanding trade books for children are rolling off printing presses with each publishing season.... The boom in children's books is undoubtedly the major publishing trend of the late 20th century. (Cullinan, 1992a, p. 1)

These two forces, the prominent use of children's literature in school and home and the proliferation of children's books in the publishing world, are reflected in the Children's Choices project, a joint venture of the Children's Book Council (CBC) and the International Reading Association (IRA), in which 10,000 children across the United States annually select 100 favorite books. It is the only booklist of its scope and kind selected entirely by children.

A primary goal of elementary and middle school teachers as well as administrators, parents, and caregivers is to engage children in reading for enjoyment and for the advancement of their reading ability. If we can engage children in reading books that interest them, their love of reading as well as their reading ability will improve (Guthrie &

Wigfield, 1997). The 25th anniversary of the Children's Choices project and the dawn of a new century seem to be a propitious moment for celebrating the books that have been Children's Choices. These events provide an opportunity to compare the development of this project with developments in literacy and literacy instruction, and to reflect on research and writing in the field of literacy instruction as they relate to children's literature and reading. *Celebrating Children's Choices: 25 Years of Children's Favorite Books* highlights the variety of Children's Choices books and provides teachers with new insights into the use of these books with children. Although it is intended for classroom teachers, *Celebrating Children's Choices* will be useful to librarians as well as reading specialists.

The Children's Choices Project

The project is the result of a partnership between CBC and IRA, whose visions for literacy intersect. Both organizations strive to put children's literature in the hands of children. A description of each organization shows this mutual interest:

> IRA is a nonprofit educational organization whose members include classroom and reading teachers, school administrators and supervisors, parents, college/university faculty, and others who are dedicated to improving reading instruction and promoting literacy worldwide.
>
> CBC is a nonprofit organization encouraging the use and enjoyment of books and related literacy materials for young people. Its members are U.S. publishers and packagers of trade books for children and young adults, and producers of book-related materials for children. (Children's Choices for 1998, p. 1)

The partnership began in 1969 with the formation of the CBC/IRA Liaison Committee. The liaison was logical, given the mutual interest of CBC and IRA in children and reading. The first liaison committee met with the goal of increasing the use of children's literature in the classroom and addressing the "concerns of reading teachers and children's book publishers" (Classroom Choices: Children's Trade Books 1974, p. 1). The first list, titled "Classroom Choices," was compiled in 1974 and first appeared in *The Reading Teacher*, November 1975. The focus was on supplying an "evaluative list of current children's trade books for the classroom teacher" (p. 1).

Since its inception, Children's Choices has matured along with the fields of literacy, literacy instruction, and children's literature. Its scope and outreach have widened to recognize the many influences on children's literacy development. The intended audience of the list has expanded to include "not only teachers, librarians, and administrators, but also parents, grandparents, caregivers, and everyone who wishes to encourage young people to read for pleasure" (Children's Choices for 1998, p. 1).

Each year five review teams, representing different regions of the United States, oversee the distribution of more than 700 titles to be evaluated by 2,000 children in their respective regions. The books are sent to the review teams by children's book publishers who are members of the Children's Book Council. Each publisher may select up to seven titles (excluding reprints) or 10% of children's books they published the preceding year (whichever is smaller) (P. Quint, personal communication, May 1998). The books are read to or by the children who then vote by marking a ballot answering the question, "Did you like this book? Yes or No." Answers are counted and tabulated to arrive at the top 100 choices for the year. Review team members then write brief annotations for each Children's Choices book and group them by ages. The annotated list is published annually in the October issue of *The Reading Teacher*.

History of Children's Choices Project

Interestingly, the history and development of the Children's Choices project such as organization and selection of the list, expansion of its aims and uses, and the development of a logo coincided with many of the developments in the field of literacy instruction and children's literature such as the proliferation of children's literature being published and the increased use of children's literature in school literacy curricula.

The Proliferation of Children's Literature

The increased number of children's books within the last quarter century has been phenomenal. During the 1970s, more than 2,000 children's trade books were published yearly. In the 1980s, the number of titles increased from nearly 3,000 to over 4,500. In 1992, the Children's Choices list qualified the eligibility criteria for books to be considered for the list, which excluded reprints; therefore it is difficult to tell how many reprints were included during 1978 to 1991. Nevertheless, a tremendous growth in the publication of children's trade books occurred. New publishing companies were formed and new divisions within companies increased, which resulted in increased sales of children's books.

Broadening the Base: Organization and Book Selection

In the beginning of the Children's Choices project, two trends suggested a top-down model of committee organization and book selection. First, there was leadership by university professors. The review committee was composed of five review teams, each headed by a children's literature specialist at a university and one or two classroom teachers who worked with other teachers and children. Perhaps this organizational arrangement was the result of those who organized the project, but it also seems to reflect higher education as the purveyor and the source of knowledge. By 1980 the teams reflected more representation of school personnel. It appears that teams moved to a more horizontal arrangement with the leadership of supervisors and teachers from elementary schools. Today both the committee and the review teams contain a mixture of university and school personnel. Neither the CBC-IRA Liaison Committee nor the review teams require university personnel in a leadership position.

The lessening of university leadership seemed to parallel the whole language movement, which encouraged teachers to trust themselves, to have confidence in their abilities, and to delight in the excitement of their learners (Atwell, 1987, 1998; Routman, 1988, 1991, 2000). At the same time, many in the research community began to trust teachers in terms of action research arising and occurring in the classroom, which was seen as a fertile ground. Goodman (1992) calls the whole language movement

> a coming of age of educational practice, a new era in which practitioners are informed professionals acting on the basis of an integrated and articulated theory.... The differences in whole language classrooms come about because teachers are not relying on gurus and experts to tell them what to do. They make their own decisions and build their own implementations based on their own understandings. (p. 47)

The second trend that showed a broadening of the base was the selection process. In 1973, the CBC-IRA Liaison established a subcommittee to select and review titles from the current year's selection of children's books, which were appropriate to classroom curricula and to reading programs. The distinguishing feature was "that the books would be ones that children had actually enjoyed." As books were read aloud, read alone, introduced by the teacher or selected by the students themselves, or used to initiate or follow up class activities, teachers carefully observed and kept informal accounts of the children's responses (Classroom Choices: Children's Trade Books 1974, pp. 1–2).

In the 1980s educators no longer selected the whole list. Instead, they composed a list from which children voted for their favorite books. Children's votes were counted at the IRA Annual Convention and the Children's Choices list was determined." A title change from Classroom Choices to Children's Choices indicated that children's input was increasing. In the 1990s the preselected list was eliminated. Publishers submitted 650 of 3,000 eligible books, excluding reprints, directly to the five review teams (Children's Choices for 1992). Children read or listened to a book and marked ballots. Numerical equivalents of reader responses were tabulated, and approximately 100 books were selected as the Children's Choices booklist each year.

The selection of titles showed a movement from the input of children to complete selection of the titles by the children involved in the project. This trend paralleled the transfer of many instructional decisions to children. Children needed and were given time to read and write, as well as a choice of what to read and write (Graves, 1983). Even advocates of the skills-oriented side of the literacy learning continuum encouraged more reading to produce better, more fluent readers (Beck, 1998; Samuels, Schermer, & Reinking, 1992). Teachers trusted their students to select and read materials of interest, which became an integral part of their reading programs. Teachers showed their confidence in the 10,000 children who read books for the Children's Choices project by exposing their classes to the books from the Children's Choices list. In sum, the Children's Choices project reflected shifts in literacy learning and instruction directly to children.

The Aim and Uses of the List

A striking feature of the Children's Choices lists is the broadening of the targeted audience, reflecting the growing realization that a whole community is involved in children's literacy development (Campbell 1998; Glazer & Burke 1994; Neuman & Roskos 1998; Strickland & Morrow, 1989). The popularity of Jim Trelease (1989, 1995), whose books about reading aloud to children and whose presentations delighted parents and teachers, attests to the wide interest in obtaining children's books for home reading.

The developing view of the family and community involvement in children's literacy coincided with the increasing use, and often sole use, of children's literature in the literacy curriculum of schools. Professional books that included suggestions for using children's literature in the classroom gained wide appeal (Cullinan, 1987, 1992b; Gambrell & Almasi, 1996; Roser & Martinez, 1995), as did those that contained annotated titles and age suggestions (Gunning, 1998; McClure & Kristo, 1994).

The Children's Choices Logo

The Children's Choices logo first appeared on the reprint from *The Reading Teacher*, October 1986. It was designed by Tomie dePaola, an ideal artist to represent a booklist chosen by children. As an author and illustrator of children's books for several decades, he represents both the writing and the artistic aspects of creating children's books. The logo for Children's Choices seems to tell it all, featuring a young boy and a girl sitting back to back, each absorbed in a book. Behind them are stacks of books waiting to be read. The children in the logo demonstrate the goal of the Children's Choices project: to bring children and books together. DePaola's books are well represented on the Children's Choices lists, which have included *Watch Out for the Chicken Feet in Your Soup* (1974), *Bill and Pete* (1978), *Pancakes for Breakfast* (1978), *The Comic Adventures of Old Mother Hubbard and Her Dog* (1981), *Fin M'Coul, the Giant of Knockmany Hill* (1981), *Tomie dePaola's Mother Goose* (1985), *Little Grunt and the Big Egg: A Prehistoric Fairy Tale* (1990), and *Bill and Pete to the Rescue* (1998).

Continuity With Some Change

Although many aspects of the Children's Choices project have changed over the years with developments in literacy instruction and children's literature, the most enduring and significant aspect is the partnership between CBC and IRA. Despite disagreements in the literacy community about how to teach reading and the place of phonics instruction and whole language in the reading program, it is refreshing to note that publishers, researchers, educators, and parents agree that the use of children's literature advances the love of reading and the improvement of reading (Flippo, 1999).

Selection of Books for *Celebrating Children's Choices*

How did we select from among the 2,500 books that have appeared over the years of the Children's Choices project? The challenge was great, and the following criteria were applied to the selection process:

1. The titles include a sampling from each age group among which Children's Choices were divided annually in *The Reading Teacher*: beginning independent reader (ages 5–6), young reader (ages 6–8), intermediate or middle reader (ages 8–10), and advanced or older reader (ages 10–13).

2. The titles represent a sampling from the 25 years of the Children's Choices project. Most of the titles come from the 1990s, several from the 1980s, and a few from the 1970s.

3. The older titles have stood the test of time in popularity, and have created exciting instructional uses in the classroom, as presented in this publication.

4. The newer titles present unique and interesting elements, such as a contemporary topic, an intriguing illustration, a current message, or a stretch across grades.

5. Many of the titles form a natural content area connection. For example, in Chapter 3 and Chapter 4, *The Magic School Bus Blows Its Top: A Book About Volcanoes* and *A River Ran Wild* connect with science. In Chapter 5, four titles by Jean Fritz connect with social studies.

6. The titles have been used in compelling, concrete ways in classrooms with activities that are easy for teachers to duplicate and use immediately, including charts and diagrams.

In *Celebrating Children's Choices*, the titles are grouped according to the grade or grade ranges in which they were used. We encourage teachers not to be bound by the grade levels presented, but to reach across the grades in using the titles and instructional ideas. Several of the teachers we describe present a unique perspective on a book's use. For example, in Chapter 5, *Tops and Bottoms*, a title for younger children, is used to teach antonyms in middle school. In Chapter 3, *Katie K. Whale* provides a school-wide theme stretching from kindergarten through third grade.

Contents of *Celebrating Children's Choices*

This chapter has described the Children's Choices project and traced its development throughout the years. The history of Children's Choices takes on added significance when comparisons, connections, and parallels are drawn to the development of literacy instruction, views of reading and children's literature, and the relationships among professionals. Chapter 2 reviews recent research relating to the use of children's literature and identifies strands of research that seem to support the kinds of literacy activities that will be presented in subsequent chapters. The remaining chapters are grouped by the grade levels in which teachers and students interacted with the featured Children's Choices books. Diverse classrooms are featured, representing public, private, and parochial schools in both urban and suburban areas. The section on each book opens with the annotation that appeared in *The Reading Teacher* the year it appeared on the list, followed by a brief outline of the instructional activities described in detail.

Chapter 3 features descriptions of early elementary classrooms, kindergarten through Grade 2 or 3 (Grade 3 is included in this section when combined instructionally with the lower grades). Chapter 4 features middle elementary grades, Grades 3 and 4. Chapter 5 features older readers, Grade 5 and up. Although we respected the grade levels of the teachers who used the books, the books should not be thought of as mutually exclusive to these grade levels. The examples provided should demonstrate how versatile these books are across grade levels. Finally, the Afterword draws some conclusions and spurs us forward into 21st-century literacy.

A Look Ahead

What will children's literature bring us in the 21st century? Will the explosion of children's books continue? Will children's literature be the primary sources of reading material in the classroom? Will the renewed interest in phonics and skills-oriented teaching change the whole language focus of the last two decades?

We hope that the positive trends will continue. We hope that the involvement of families and caregivers in sharing books with children will grow. Our goal is to aid children's literacy development and spark children's interest in reading. Books chosen by children provide the motivation to read. An increase in reading leads to improved reading that motivates children to read more, and the cycle continues. We know it works. Let's keep a good thing going and enjoy Children's Choices books with the children in our classrooms and in our lives.

Children's Books by Tomie dePaola

Watch out for the chicken feet in your soup. (1974). New York: Simon & Schuster.

Bill and Pete. (1978). New York: Putnam.

Pancakes for breakfast. (1978). San Diego: Harcourt.

The comic adventures of old Mother Hubbard and her dog. (1981). San Diego: Harcourt.

Fin M'Coul, the giant of Knockmany Hill. (1981). New York: Holiday House.

Tomie dePaola's Mother Goose. (1985). New York: Putnam.

Little Grunt and the big egg: A prehistoric fairy tale. (1990). New York: Holiday House.

Bill and Pete to the rescue. (1998). New York: Putnam.

Children's Literature in the Curriculum and at Home

Literacy is developed by engaging children in meaningful literacy events (reading and discussing favorite books, writing letters for relevant purposes and audiences) and in so doing helping them (through demonstrations, support, practice, celebration, and evaluation) become better readers, writers, speakers, and thinkers. (Routman, 2000, p. 19)

The use of children's literature in the school and the home seems so well established that one might wonder why such a chapter is included in a book celebrating Children's Choices. There are two reasons: (1) to set a theoretical and research basis for the subsequent activities that focus on specific books, and (2) to identify major strands in the professional literature and demonstrate the relevance of the Children's Choices lists in meeting the findings and suggestions of research.

The following strands, while not exhaustive, will be addressed briefly and their sources identified so that they may be pursued in more detail:

- The Importance of Using Children's Literature
- The Content Area Connection
- The Comprehension Revolution
- The Integration of Listening, Speaking, Reading, and Writing
- The Importance of Talk and Discussion
- The Importance of Early Literacy
- The Use of Children's Literature for At-Risk Learners
- A Variety of Genres
- The Affective and Attitude Components of Literacy

The Importance of Using Children's Literature

It is interesting to note that as recently as 1987 Cullinan devotes considerable attention to the rationale for using children's literature in the classroom. What we now accept that the idea that all reading programs have some—and usually an extensive—literature component has not always been so. Cullinan suggests the power of a good story to teach comprehension and capture the reader's interest. She reminds us of the importance of teacher attitude and enthusiasm in inspiring students and stresses the importance of reading aloud to students. She echoes so many others in saying, "students who read a lot become fluent readers" (Cullinan, 1987, p. 13).

We have come to accept that children need to be immersed in literature from the earliest years and that we need to make classrooms rich in literacy events (Huck & Kerstetter, 1987). The suggestion that wide reading, which means spending significant amounts of time reading from a variety of genres and materials, leads to more and better reading resembles the chicken and the egg question: Which comes first? It would seem that we need to motivate and support children in their reading so that they can read widely; the sequence is then set in motion. A key component of the support is finding books of interest to children so they may reap the benefits of wide reading (Gunning, 1998).

The Children's Choices list meets the need for providing literature suggestions for teachers. It is the only list of its scope and size that contains solely children's choices of favorite books. It seems a likely source for educators and families to use in providing books of interest to children. Furthermore, its division into age levels makes it easy to reference.

The Content Area Connection

Although the use of children's literature to teach the language arts has received much attention in the last 20 years (Strickland, 1987), the use of children's trade books in the content areas has followed quickly and continues to develop (Cullinan, 1992a; Langer, 1995). Content area teachers, particularly in upper grade levels, may be reluctant to make time for children's trade books in an already full curriculum. Reading and language arts educators, however, see value in instilling more personal interaction with the content through the use of trade books. A personal response to content area information can have a more lasting value for students than getting through a certain amount of content material, as some content teachers are discovering. The number of trade books with a content area connection is increasing in both publication and classroom use (*More Teachers Favorite Books for Kids; Teachers' Choices 1994–1996*).

An added impetus for using children's literature in the content areas may result from interest in developing children's multiple intelligences. Based on Gardner's (1983) theory of multiple intelligences, teachers realize that they need to assist children in their specific areas of ability by providing learning activities that tap into multiple areas. Furthermore, many teachers have sought to develop multiple intelligences in all students through instruction that provides for several ways of expressing learning (Gardner, 1983; Gardner & Hatch, 1989). Gardner's intelligences include verbal-linguistic, logical-mathematical, spatial, musical, artistic, kinesthetic, interpersonal, and intrapersonal, to which has been added another, naturalist.

The Children's Choices lists contain books that integrate well with content areas and enable children to become personally involved in the content. Children's trade books evoke the reader's aesthetic stance, which contrasts with the efferent stance (Rosenblatt, 1985) common in content areas. The efferent stance involves reading for information. On the other hand, an aesthetic stance involves reading to feel, to relive, and to become part of the experience. Although teachers in the past tended to focus on the efferent stance, more and more attention is paid now to developing the aesthetic stance, even in content area reading. Books about the arts and humanities provide an excellent opportunity to experience the aesthetic stance. Appreciation of art, music, and drama, developed from reading children's books, creates personal interactions with books and experiences (Gaines, 1992; Sebesta, 1987, 1992; Sinatra, 1994).

The efferent and aesthetic stances are not limited to the arts and humanities. Nonfiction trade books can play an important role in developing concepts in social studies, geography, and science. By encouraging creative and personal responses to books, teachers are reinforcing the concepts in content areas and supporting oral- and written-language growth. Through teacher read-alouds, the reading-writing connection, and the use of picture books, biographies, and informational books, students develop a deeper appreciation for and understanding of the content (Freeman & Person, 1992). (Kathleen O'Neill's use of *The River Ran Wild* in Chapter 4 provides a striking example.)

In social studies, students' identification with characters, times, places, and situations enriches the social studies program (Carter & Abrahamson, 1992). This is illustrated with the books by Jean Fritz described in Chapter 5, which complement a class theme, The American Revolution. Science becomes real when insects, animals, and nature are studied through trade books (Lapp & Flood, 1992), as illustrated in the weather lesson and the volcano lesson in Chapter 3. Math comes alive and becomes fun when combined with children's literature (Cohn & Wendt, 1992), as evident in the whale lessons in Chapter 3. However, with the proliferation and possibilities of using trade books in content areas, Langer (1995) would caution that use of literature across the curriculum may not result in children seeing alternative ways to view their understanding from a literary perspective. Teachers must be sure not to lose the literary value of the trade book in content area use (Richardson, 2000).

Throughout their existence, the Children's Choices lists have always included a variety of genres, including informational selections, biography, and historical fiction, which offer content area connections. As the number and quality of informational books have increased, so have the number of these titles on the Children's Choices lists. The lists provide teachers with alternative ways to teach content and bring that content alive through quality trade books that have already attracted children. The books allow readers to take an aesthetic stance while still obtaining information.

The Comprehension Revolution

A significant aspect of contemporary literacy instruction involves comprehension. In the late 1970s and early 1980s, a strong movement revolutionized reading instruction by placing maximum emphasis on comprehension. The comprehension revolution resulted in theory and practice that affect reading instructional practice today. Schema theorists examined the impact of a reader's schemata—knowledge already stored in memory—in that reader's comprehension. Rumelhart (1980) defines schemata as "the building blocks of cognition upon which all information processing depends" (p. 33). Anderson and Pearson (1984) explain further:

> One aspect of particular importance to reading comprehension is the issue of how a reader's schemata...function in the process of interpreting new information and allowing it to enter and become part of a knowledge store…. It is this interaction of new information with old knowledge that we mean when we use the term *comprehension*. (p. 255)

The implication of schema theory affected the teaching of both content area text, also known as informational or expository text, and narrative or story material. Semantic mapping (Smith & Johnson, 1980) and story mapping, based on story grammar (Stein & Glenn, 1979, 1982), resulted in a multitude of instructional strategies to aid comprehension. Semantic mapping, also called webbing, remains in wide use for teaching concepts and vocabulary as do variations of story mapping strategies for the classroom (Vacca, Vacca, & Gove, 2000).

In addition to the schema theorists and their influence on the teaching of comprehension was the growing recognition of reading as a process in which meaning is built, much as a builder constructs a house. A commonly recognized definition of reading is the process of constructing meaning through the dynamic interaction of reader, text, and context (Michigan Reading Association, 1986). Factors that influence the reader include background knowledge, skills, metacognitive strategy use, attitude toward reading, and interest in the reading material. Strategies such as the Directed Reading-Thinking Activity (DRTA), with its predict-read-prove sequence (Stauffer, 1975), and What I Know, What I Want to Know, and What I Learned (K-W-L) (Ogle, 1986) and its more recent counterpart, K-W-L-Q, in which the Q stands for Questions That Remain (Schmidt, 1999), engage the reader in activating prior knowledge and arousing interest in reading material. Question-Answer Relationships (QAR) (Raphael, 1986) with four levels of comprehension—Right There, Think and Search, On My Own, and more recently added Author and You—engage a reader in identifying sources of answers to questions within a text. They get at the heart of metacognition (thinking about thinking), in which a reader consciously examines the comprehension process and selects appropriate strategies.

In Chapters 3–5, teachers give attention to comprehension. There are variations of semantic webbing and story mapping with Children's Choices books, as well as the DRTA, K-W-L, and QAR. In addition, teachers offer their own charts for examining prior knowledge, relating past and present knowledge, and comparing and contrasting as one aspect of critical thinking (Beyer, 1988; Kneedler, 1985).

The Integration of Listening, Speaking, Reading, and Writing

The whole language movement stressed the integration of listening, speaking, reading, and writing as a simple, natural phenomenon. This connectedness, the bringing of "reading, writing, listening, and speaking together so that each feeds off and feeds into the other" (Flippo, 1999, p. 23), requires a strong children's literature component in literacy instruction. Recently, two additional components are often included in a literacy framework: "viewing and visually representing," which offer children "endless opportunities to communicate" (Hennings, 2000, p. 11). Chapters 3, 4, and 5 provide examples of teachers using viewing and visually representing in literacy connections such as connecting a video to a book, using the Internet, using the computer for word processing, and creating art work.

All components of literacy are learned simultaneously and continue to develop in concert with one another in home settings and in the classroom. Family involvement facilitates literate interactions so that literacy develops in real situations, in and out of school, and in functional settings (Glazer & Burke, 1994). Karen De Young provides a unique example in Chapter 5 of using a picture book with her middle school students to teach a skill, then helping her students share books with younger students and with family members.

An excellent example of the reading-writing connection in schools is the use of book clubs. Book clubs provide a natural means for the reading-writing connection in their four program components: community share, reading, writing, and small student-led discussion groups (McMahon & Raphael, 1997). In the following chapters, several teachers use elements of the book club.

Children's Choices lists provide a ready source of books to use in developing the listening, speaking, reading, and writing connection because they have proven their interest to children. The titles are a natural source for classroom literacy activities, book club selections, journal responses, classroom drama, sharing in small groups or in the author's chair, and for reading aloud by teacher and students, as the following chapters show.

The Importance of Talk and Discussion

The importance of the oral language component and the nature of oral interactions continue to receive attention in the scholarly and research literature, which often focuses on book conversations. Children should be encouraged to talk about and share their reading in a variety of ways (Flippo, 1999).

Book talks are more than questions asked by adults and answered by children. A collaborative environment is needed, one with give-and-take among the participants, each of whom contributes thoughts, ideas, feelings, and responses (Almasi, 1996). Discussions can occur with emergent readers; even young children can participate in book talk. Martinez and Roser (1995) remind us, "The best book talk is not launched when a teacher fires a set of questions designed to monitor readers' grasp of the storyline...rather, it occurs when the story itself and children's honest, spontaneous reactions are central to the discussion" (1995, p. 33). Yet questions can serve as a springboard for discussion as several teachers demonstrate in Chapters 3 and 4.

Book talks suggest a dialogue rather than a question-and-answer session (Gambrell & Almasi, 1996). Dialogue among readers and teachers enables a deeper interpretation of a story's content and structure (Eeds & Peterson, 1995). Children's talk can be turned into a valuable classroom currency (Cullinan, 1995), which is what appears to have been done in the Book Club Program (McMahon & Raphael, 1997), which makes extensive use of oral language. McMahon and Raphael stress the need for discussions to occur around meaningful literacy activities and interactions about literature, not around texts created simply to teach reading.

Once again, the Children's Choices lists seem to be a natural choice for furthering the oral language component of a classroom. They represent books chosen by children ages 5 to 13 as favorites, which makes them likely sources for book conversations among students, students and teachers, and children and parents. All the classroom accounts in the following chapters make extensive use of oral language.

The Importance of Early Literacy

The concept of literacy as an emerging set of knowledge and skills that occurs in very young children has been strongly supported by Marie Clay (1975). She believes that children accumulate literacy as they move about their preschool settings. By dispelling the notion of reading readiness in which a child has to attain certain competencies to be ready to learn to read, Clay has created the understanding that children are involved in aspects of literacy development from birth.

In recent years there has been much research and writing on young children's literacy development. The involvement in a variety of literacy activities at home, in day care, and in preschool prepares a child for the beginning reading situation in school (Strickland & Morrow, 1989). The connection between the development of language and thought, earlier theorized and expounded on by the Russian psychologist Vygotsky (1978), found new attention among literacy educators. Thought and language are developmentally intertwined. Literacy develops in real literacy situations in and out of school (Glazer & Burke, 1994) where the need to think and communicate occur naturally. Thus, the connection among listening, speaking, reading, and writing was stressed even among young children as early literacy researchers proposed the concurrent learning of these language components.

One of the most important aspects of early literacy involvement is reading aloud to children (Glazer & Burke, 1994). Both professional and popular literature has advocated the need to read aloud to children. The shared book experience (Holdaway, 1979), involving a big book on display to the class while the teacher reads aloud, and the use of predictable stories, such as Bill Martin Jr's *Brown Bear, Brown Bear, What Do You See?*, brought attention to sharing books with young children. Jim Trelease (1989, 1995), in *The Read Aloud Handbook*, made suggestions about how to read aloud to children and how to involve them in reading, and included titles for reading aloud.

Recent research suggests the active nature of children's involvement in stories. It reflects the social constructivist theory that readers, listeners, and writers—even very young children—construct their own meaning. Literacy activities that enable children to construct their own meanings might involve, for example, a child as the storyteller. The need exists for a range of books that support children in various ways and for young children's classrooms to be rich literacy environments (Campbell, 1998).

Neuman and Roskos (1998) use the term *early literacy* to reflect the continuum of reading and writing development and the wide range of individual variation among young children in developing literacy competence. They stress the importance of parent involvement and of using children's literature in early literacy development. Children's literature provides models of literary language and structures, and opportunities to talk about and understand stories, to develop vocabulary knowledge, and to construct story meanings (McGee, 1998).

The attention to literacy for young children includes specific suggestions for appropriate books for children ages 3–8 (Slaughter, 1993). Such published lists are valuable but the books have usually been selected by adults, often as a result of experiences using the particular books with young children (Trelease, 1989, 1995). Children's Choices offers a distinct advantage in that it is chosen entirely by children. Given the importance of children's literature for young children, the Children's Choices categories of beginning independent readers (ages 5–6) and young readers (ages 6–8) are primary sources of books that delight and capture the interest of young children.

In Chapter 3, early elementary teachers use Children's Choices books because they know these books facilitate early literacy development. Teachers read aloud from them; construct listening, speaking, and writing activities from them; and start their students on a lifelong literacy journey.

The Use of Children's Literature for At-Risk Learners

Many recently published books on reading and children's literacy include a chapter on the at-risk learner. *At-risk learner* is a broad term that refers to children from environments that put them at a disadvantage for learning. The type of environment is not limited to poverty. It may include families in which "the television is used as a continual babysitter, regardless of children's socioeconomic status...also, a parent who wants to 'hurry' a child" or accelerate his or her literacy development (Vacca, Vacca, & Gove, 1995, p. 82). Children for whom English is a second language (ESL) or who have limited English proficiency (LEP) for any reason, including the primary use of diverse dialects, can be at risk. *The Literacy Dictionary: The Vocabulary of Reading and Writing* (Harris & Hodges, 1995) defines *at risk* as "referring to a person or group whose prospects for success are marginal or worse" (p. 13).

Allington and Walmsley (1995) discuss at-risk learners by challenging educators and schools to re-examine their literacy and remedial programs to accommodate diversity among students. The authors stress the complexity of assuring that all children become literate and inform us that there is no quick and easy way to accomplish this. Prominent within the successful programs and remedial approaches they describe is the presence of children's literature. In another study, in the self-selected reading block of a four-block schedule, at-risk children chose to read trade books from a wide variety of books and other reading material in two schools with a large population of minority children and children who qualified for free or reduced lunch (Hall, Prevatte, &

Cunningham, 1995). In an early intervention program (Taylor, Short, Shearer, & Frye, 1995), popular children's books were identified and arranged into four groups that represented progressively longer books. In a rural area with many children living in poverty conditions (Walp & Walmsley, 1995), the authors wanted their remedial program to reflect genuine literacy activities. To that end they immersed all their students in a wide range of literature and genres across the grades: "The first thing [they] did was to use full-length literature as the basis for all remedial instruction" (Walp & Walmsley, 1995, p. 185). In short, children's literature is a primary source of reading material for all students, including at-risk learners.

Several of the classrooms described in the following chapters include at-risk learners who are immersed in literature. In Chapter 5 the account of *Philip Hall Likes Me. I Reckon Maybe* reaches out to a multiracial urban community. The use of four Jean Fritz books with fifth graders enables the teachers to meet varying reading instructional levels.

The use of children's literature for ESL learners has also been documented. Nurss and Hough (1992) reviewed the literature on ESL programs and found extensive use of whole texts and oral reading of picture books that match language with illustrations and repeat language patterns. They also found that culturally familiar content improves comprehension; for instance, when the passage matched the cultural experiences of the children and when the text's narrative structure was consistent and predictable. In Chapter 5, *Seedfolks* uses an urban, multiethnic setting to reach diverse students. Its short chapters maintain attention and set up interest for what will follow.

In one study of a bilingual kindergarten, collaborative story talk based on children's literature facilitated language and reading development (Battle, 1995). The author found that frequent exposure to children's literature books in which second language learners could connect and associate with the story led to discussion to make meaning of the story. Battle reports that the students were motivated to communicate by their connection to quality stories.

It would seem that culturally diverse and sensitive books that relate to children's personal experiences, books that are well written and have predictable language patterns and good stories, and books that are of interest to the readers who read or listen to them are essential for at-risk literacy learners. The Children's Choices booklists meet these criteria by including folktales from many cultures, stories by diverse authors and about diverse populations, and books with predictable language and story structure. The fact that the books are selected by such a divergent group of children seems to suggest that these books are of high interest and appeal to all children who read them.

A Variety of Genres

Children's literature is a rich source of different genres of literature. Children's early introduction to books is through the genre of picture books, and much research has supported and advocated the use of picture books with children. Gunning (1998) provides an exhaustive list of picture books, grouping them by reading level from picture level (a single word or phrase depicted with an illustration) up through level 2A (up to 20 lines of text per page). He further indicates the theme of each, such as animals, counting, or friendship. Kiefer (1995) sees more than a casual enjoyment of picture books by suggesting we look at picture books as art forms that may result in different aesthetic response forms (Rosenblatt, 1985) among children.

Multicultural books, recently listed as a separate genre by some in the field of children's literature, may actually include a variety of genres (for example, Hennings, 1997, 2000). Bishop (1992) suggests the use of folklore, realistic fiction, and poetry from various cultures to extend understandings and attitudes important to life in a multicultural society. Understanding divergent cultures can change our perspectives of ourselves and the world. A broad perspective and multicultural understanding take on increasing significance as our world continues to expand. Clothing, customs, holidays, language, food, and traditions can be studied through a variety of genres with a multicultural theme or context: informational books, traditional literature, picture books, biographies, and historical fiction. In fact, any genre that treats a multicultural topic with respect, appreciation, and sensitivity is worthy of classroom study. In Chapter 4 the use of Cinderella tales fosters an appreciation for cultural diversity as well as the connectedness of the human experience.

The growing use of the informational genre is addressed in *Using Nonfiction Trade Books in the Elementary Classroom* (Freeman & Person, 1992), an entire book devoted to this topic. After distinguishing their use of the term *nonfiction* from the common Dewey Decimal classification of informational books that includes poetry or folklore, the authors point out the many uses of nonfiction in the classroom in various content areas: social studies, science, and the fine arts.

Other writers have focused on specific genres and content areas. Science fiction and high fantasy have captured the interest of students and facilitated the development of higher level thinking skills (Greenlaw & McIntosh, 1987). Realistic fiction and historical fiction have stimulated laughter, wonder, sadness, curiosity, or fear as upper elementary students interacted with characters (Monson, 1987). The use of historical fiction, biography, and informational books can make the past come alive by personalizing history and exploring the human experience, evoking a connection to the past. Chapters 4 and 5 include titles in several of these genres.

Poetry, once thought to belong to the literature curriculum of the high school, has reached the elementary level through such authors as Shel Silverstein, Jack Prelutsky, and Eloise Greenfield, who have made poetry real and fun for children. Perhaps the foremost proponent of poetry in the children's literature curriculum is Bernice Cullinan, who provides a multitude of teaching suggestions for using poetry to teach social studies, science, math, reading, writing, and oral language (Cullinan, Scala, & Schroder, 1995). As one of the founders of the Children's Choices lists, Cullinan supported poetry inclusions, and the lists even contained a poetry category for a few years. In Chapter 5, Lobel's *The Book of Pigericks* engages students in a lighthearted approach to poetry, and the use of biopoems from two Jean Fritz books expands poetry into a content area.

The Children's Choices lists reflect children's interests in all of the genres. A good mix of the genres is represented each year, which gives teachers the opportunity to select books according to children's personal genre preferences or classroom needs.

The Affective and Attitude Components of Literacy

A final strand to consider in children's literature as it relates to literacy instruction is the affective, feeling, or attitude component, often referred to as motivation to read. There are children who know how to read competently and capably, but who choose not to read. The affective aspects of reading have traditionally not received the attention given to the cognitive aspects and have often been neglected (Cramer & Castle, 1994). The classroom environment builds positive reading attitudes by surrounding children with a variety of books that they can select to take home that cover a wide range of interests (Cramer, 1994).

Children's attraction to a book can often be traced to the book's ability to grab their interest. Wigfield (1997) found that children's reading is influenced by children's absorption of the characters and the plot of a story. Hynds (1997) cites a reluctant eighth-grade reader who attributes a Stephen King novel with getting him hooked on reading; he went on to engage in literary criticism. Pressley (1998) suggests that motivation to read is influenced by factors such as self-efficacy, a belief in one's competence, time to read, and a choice of what to read.

By providing material of interest to children, the Children's Choices lists serve a crucial role in motivating children to read. The children who vote on the titles represent the ages, interests, abilities, and diversity of children across the United States. As part of the voting process, these children are provided with time to read and a choice of what to read (Graves, 1983, 1994) so that they can pick interesting books at their own levels of competence.

Summary

This chapter has set a theoretical and research basis for subsequent chapters and has demonstrated the relevance of the Children's Choices books in meeting these research findings. Because the use of children's literature in literacy instruction has become such a prominent component of most elementary classrooms, teachers actively search for information about appropriate, engaging literature to use in their classrooms and that has proven its popularity with children. Children's Choices books provide an excellent opportunity to engage children in exciting literacy events that have been selected by the premiere authorities in motivating children to read: the children themselves.

Books Used With
YOUNGER READERS

COWS CAN'T FLY

CLOUDY WITH A CHANCE OF MEATBALLS

KATIE K. WHALE

THE DOORBELL RANG

THE MAGIC SCHOOL BUS
BLOWS ITS TOP

BUNNICULA

MISS NELSON IS MISSING

Books Used With Younger Readers

IMAGINE THE IMPOSSIBLE WITH COWS CAN'T FLY

(written and illustrated by David Milgrim)

Inspired by a young boy's drawing of cows in the air, a herd of cows takes flight. All of the adults are too busy looking down, so only the boy and his dog enjoy the flight. Realizing that cows can fly, the boy wonders what might be next!

Children's Choices for 1999. Reprinted from *The Reading Teacher*, October 1999.

 Activities for This Book

Book Buddies

Teacher reading aloud

Rhyming patterns

Chart what we know and what we want to know

Chart fact and fiction

Animal fantasy statement

Illustrate the statement

Write a poem or story

Wacky Animal Share

Present to an audience

Sharing milk and cow-shaped cookies

Word Work

Cow research on the Internet

Flavorful Flavored Milk Recipes

Field trip

At an East Coast elementary school, kindergarten teacher Bradford High and second-grade teacher Christine Pingley consider themselves literacy partners because they share similar beliefs about literacy. They believe in establishing a firm, early reading-writing connection with their young readers. Brad and Christine know that a strong start to literacy development will benefit children throughout their schooling, a belief with widespread support among teachers (Flippo, 1999). They also believe in immersing children in literature by making their classrooms stimulating literacy environments (Huck & Kerstetter, 1987). They have seen the power of a good story as it works its magic on young children, and they are committed to providing a literacy environment that encourages students' spontaneous reactions to literature (Martinez & Roser, 1995).

Toward the end of summer as they prepare for a new school year, Brad and Christine look for new titles of children's books to share with their students. They consult the Children's Choices lists because they know these titles have proven popular with children the same ages as their students. With this in mind, Brad and Christine discover a delightful, captivating, and somewhat unusual 1999 Children's Choices book, *Cows Can't Fly* by David Milgrim. They envision many reading-writing connections they can make and the excitement they can generate with activities connected to this book. They appreciate the book's use of fantasy and dreams that appeal to children, as they know from having used *Dreams* by Peter Spier and *Bobo's Dream*, a classic by Martha Alexander, with their previous classes. They especially like the visionary aspect of *Cows Can't Fly* with its message that anything may be possible.

Book Buddy Program

Brad and Christine want their students to get an early start on literature conversations. They believe that young learners need to engage in collaborative activites in which they can share reading and writing as well as their thoughts, feelings, and reactions to children's books. They have found that their kindergartners and second graders can indeed interact with each other over books. However, they recognize the emerging nature of literacy knowledge and skills as it develops in young children (Clay, 1975), and they see evidence each year of the wide range of literacy competence in their kindergartners and second graders. To further their students' enjoyment of literature and literacy development, Brad and Christine set up a Book Buddy program in which kindergartners are paired with second-grade buddies. This is the third year of their program in which the buddies meet twice a week for 30-minute periods.

Brad and Christine carefully pair the kindergartners and second graders. The second graders serve as facilitators to the kindergartners. A typical session might involve the following: The second graders read a book to the kindergartners, talk with them about the book, and then write a sentence about the book for the kindergartners to illustrate. Although the second graders are generally the "literacy experts," they are sometimes surprised at what the kindergartners can do. As Christine explains,

> A few years ago Brad had a kindergartner, Georgie, who was reading children's trade books at the fourth-grade level. Fortunately, I had a second grader who was reading much above grade level, and we were able to pair them. Obviously, we don't want second graders to be uncomfortable with a kindergartner whose skills exceed their own. We pair them very carefully after we've had a chance to observe their literacy competence for a few weeks.

It was at the end of the previous school year that the teachers used _Dreams_ and _Bobo's Dream_ to deepen the sense of story in the kindergartners and to provide writing practice for second graders. These "textless" books, consisting solely of pictures, enabled the kindergartners to dictate a brief language-experience story (Allen, 1976; Stauffer, 1970) to the second graders, who served as scribes to write down the kindergartners' words. The second graders were told to do their best in spelling the words and to spell unfamiliar words by sound. Teachers referred to this as "temporary spelling" and told the students they could later check with their teachers or the Word Wall for the conventional spelling. Word walls, posted on the classroom wall, consist of basic sight words and those with personal meaning to the students to which they can refer. In choosing the book _Cows Can't Fly_, Brad and Christine hoped to venture into more literacy activities with yet a new set of literacy adventures for their budding readers and writers.

Reading Aloud

A few weeks into the new school year, Brad and Christine tell their classes about the Book Buddy program. Both classes are excited and eager to begin, which sets a positive tone and begins a community of readers (Routman, 2000). They will begin in a group setting with reading and thinking aloud by the teachers. The kindergartners carry cards with their names and sit at tables in the cafeteria, leaving a space between them. As the second graders enter the cafeteria, they are given their kindergartners' names. They locate their kindergartners, sit beside them, and introduce themselves. Christine has prompted them with some get-acquainted conversations:

Hi. I'm _____ .

My favorite books are_____.

I have a pet _____.

I like to read books about _____. What kinds of books do you like?

Tell me about your pets or your brothers and sisters.

After about 10 minutes of get-acquainted time, Brad announces he has a book he would like to read aloud, noting the rhyming patterns in it. He reads a few sentences and discusses the rhyming patterns in the book with Christine, and he demonstrates rhyming to the students:

Brad: (reading from the book) Cows can't fly, but I don't care. One day I drew some in the air.

Christine: Say, I notice that *care* and *air* rhyme! I wonder if any kindergartners or second graders can think of other words that rhyme with these words?

Students: (calling out) Hair. Pair. Fair.

Christine: Yes. Mr. H., we surely do have some children who can rhyme here. What else would you like us to do?

Brad: I'll read the book aloud and then we'll talk about it, OK?

A chorus of "yes" and "yeah" greet his proposal. Brad reads expressively, modeling oral reading for both grades.

Following the reading, they talk about cows and make a chart of What We Know and What We Want to Know about cows (see Figure 3.1). They also make a Fact and Fiction Chart, listing the things in the story that could be true (fact) and those that are fantasy (fiction) (see Figure 3.2). Brad and Christine serve as scribes, taking down ideas from the students. They note that several kindergartners appear to be as knowledgeable about cows as some second graders and that background experiences probably contributed to their knowledge: living on a farm, having relatives who live on a farm, or coming from families who read to them or take them on trips and family excursions.

Figure 3.1
What We Know and What We Want to Know

Cows Can't Fly
by David Milgrim

What We Know About Cows	What We Want to Know About Cows
They give milk. They "moo". They're fat! They eat grass.	How they make milk. Why do they "moo"? How big can they get? Do they eat anything else?

Figure 3.2
Fact and Fiction Chart

Cows Can't Fly
by David Milgrim

True (Fact)	Fantasy (Fiction)
Cows in field munch on grass	Cows talk Cows fly

Writing Activities

When it is time for buddy work, each student pair is asked to choose an animal other than cow and write a fantasy statement about it. Brad explains:

> Fantasy statements are ones that require our imaginations and dreams, just like the boy in the story when he can see cows flying. Think of an animal and a fantasy statement. Create a statement with a good word at the end for rhyming, because we'll make these statements into rhyming poems later.

Students cleverly come up with the following:

Pigs can't sing.
Frogs can't write.
Elephants can't talk.

Using the animal fantasy statement, students work together to write and illustrate a statement. The second grader serves as scribe and the kindergartner as illustrator. Soon the cafeteria is filled with laughter and excitement as the buddies create wild fantasies for their animals.

When the pairs meet next, they work to expand the statement into a four-line rhyming poem in which the first two and the last two lines rhyme. Brad and Christine are giving the students a beginning lesson in poetry. When they finish writing, each pair presents its poem to another pair. The kindergarten students show the illustrations while the second graders read the poems. An excited, noisy, and very happy atmosphere exists as the animal fantasy statements are shared (see Figure 3.3).

Figure 3.3
Animal Fantasy Statement

Pigs can't sing.
Or do a thing
In mud all day
They like to play.

Henry

Presenting to an Audience

Brad and Christine are excited about the success of buddies writing and illustrating and decide to invite other classes to presentations. They invite the first- and third-grade students to attend a presentation of Wacky Animal Readings in the cafeteria on two different days. As they arrive, each first and third grader is assigned to a kindergarten/second-grade pair. The pairs share their fantasy statements and illustrations, followed by their poems and illustrations. So that the first and third graders can hear several presentations and the kindergarten/second-grade buddies can have several opportunities to present, Brad rings a cow bell every 5 minutes while Christine directs the visitors to the next group for a new presentation.

Brad enthusiastically reports, "The experience is fabulous for all of us. Everyone is laughing at the creative ideas the students come up with for both illustrations and writing." The gathering concludes with an expressive and enthusiastic oral reading of *Cows Can't Fly* to all three classes by Brad and Christine, and with a snack of milk and cow-shaped cookies.

Word Work

Although both teachers see an opportunity to teach about words that are important to understanding cows, milk, and milk products, they focus on different levels of word learning. They agree that the two words they want to introduce are essential, but they handle them differently. Both teachers write the words *pasteurization* and *homogenization* on their respective chalkboards, but the instruction differs.

Brad asks the students to call out any letters they may recognize from these words. He then explains the meaning of each word. He pronounces each word several times, underlining it as he does so. Although he knows these words are too difficult for most kindergartners, he feels this is an opportunity to teach important concepts and to let each child glean from this lesson the word learning that is at his or her level of competence. He goes on to print on the chalkboard the uppercase letters that correspond to the lowercase letters in these words. He has children go to the board and identify letters by asking them questions such as, Who can find and circle an *h*? Who can find the uppercase *H* that I printed?

Christine also writes the words on the chalkboard. She has her students recognize smaller words within the larger words. They discuss *Pasteur* and *pasteurize* and find the meaning in the *Scholastic Children's Dictionary* (1996): "to heat milk or another liquid to a temperature that is high enough to kill harmful bacteria" (p. 377).

They note the insertion about Louis Pasteur in the Word History box on the same dictionary page and ask to know more about him. This leads to Christine's reading aloud *The Value of Believing in Yourself: The Story of Louis Pasteur* by Spencer Johnson, and *Louis Pasteur: Young Scientist* by Francine Sabin, to her class over the next few weeks. They also look up *homogenization* and find the word *homogenize*, which the *Scholastic Children's Dictionary* defines as, "to mix the cream in milk so that it is spread evenly through the liquid and does not rise to the top" (p. 252).

Christine explains that the word is a verb, an action word, just like *pasteurize*. With the addition of *-ation*, the words become "names of something" (nouns): *pasteurization* and *homogenization*. She asks the class to find the changes in the words. They quickly see that the *-ation* ending is what makes the words different. Although Grade 2 usually does not study such difficult words in their skill work with nouns and verbs, Christine jumps on a teachable moment for what she calls "word preview."

Cow Research on the Internet

Brad and Christine decide it might be fun for students to learn more about cows. Furthermore, they are always looking for learning experiences that use technology, especially the Internet, in an instructionally sound and beneficial way. After reading a factual book about cows to the classes and adding to their What We Know and What We Want to Know charts, they take the students to the computer lab to search for information about cows on the Internet. Under the direction of the computer instructor, second graders become the mentors to the kindergartners as they find pictures and facts. The following day each pair shares with another pair during a fact exchange, and everyone is invited to suggest additions to the chart.

Treats and a Field Trip

Because the fall weather is still warm, Brad and Christine want to treat their classes to some special events. They come up with a two-part grand finale to the series of events that began with the book *Cows Can't Fly*. First they announce a special event for Friday afternoon. Parent and grandparent volunteers will help to make treats during an extended Buddy Time. There will be three groups reflecting the different treats: Apple Pie, Orange Dream, and Chocolate Fizz (see Figure 3.4, page 38). The kindergartners and second graders will choose the treat they hope to make. Three stations will be set up in the classroom, one for each treat, and the students will gather around that station for instructions.

The second activity is a visit by two classes to a local farm where students feed and milk the cows. "They really learn a lot from this hands-on field trip," say the two teachers. They recall a humorous incident when a kindergartner was boarding the bus. The child looked exhausted from her day on the farm. Christine asked if she learned a lot on her trip. The child replied, "I sure have, Mrs. Pingley. I learned that we really are lucky that cows don't fly, because if they did it would be raining milk! Yuck!"

Summary

Brad and Christine showed us many valuable literacy practices. They build the concept of Book Buddies into a community of readers and writers who share literacy experiences together. They feature children's literature as a mainstay of their literacy curriculum as they search for books that have proven their appeal to children. These teachers engage in reading and thinking aloud as they interact to present a book. Their students do skill work in context while maintaining the powerful reading-writing connection. Brad and Christine recognize the

Figure 3.4
Flavorful Flavored Milk Recipes

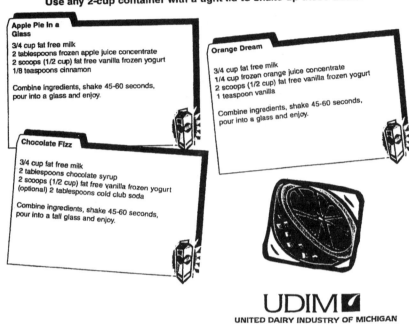

FLAVORFUL FLAVORED MILK RECIPES

Use any 2-cup container with a tight lid to shake up these treats!

Apple Pie In a Glass

3/4 cup fat free milk
2 tablespoons frozen apple juice concentrate
2 scoops (1/2 cup) fat free vanilla frozen yogurt
1/8 teaspoons cinnamon

Combine ingredients, shake 45-60 seconds, pour into a glass and enjoy.

Orange Dream

3/4 cup fat free milk
1/4 cup frozen orange juice concentrate
2 scoops (1/2 cup) fat free vanilla frozen yogurt
1 teaspoon vanilla

Combine ingredients, shake 45-60 seconds, pour into a glass and enjoy.

Chocolate Fizz

3/4 cup fat free milk
2 tablespoons chocolate syrup
2 scoops (1/2 cup) fat free vanilla frozen yogurt
(optional) 2 tablespoons cold club soda

Combine ingredients, shake 45-60 seconds, pour into a tall glass and enjoy.

UDIM
UNITED DAIRY INDUSTRY OF MICHIGAN

Provided by the United Dairy Industry of Michigan and used with permission.

value of sharing the children's written and illustrated products by bringing in an audience of first and third graders. They recognize the tremendous tool that is available in the Internet and show the children a valid purpose for its use. Finally, they appeal to children's tastes and interests by making ice cream and visiting a farm. Their students have begun an exciting literacy adventure that will last all year.

Children's Books Cited

Alexander, M. (1970). *Bobo's dream*. New York: Scholastic.

Johnson, S. (1976). *The value of believing in yourself: The story of Louis Pasteur*. La Jolla, CA: Value Communications.

Milgram, D. (1998). *Cows can't fly*. New York: Viking.
Sabin, F. (1983). *Louis Pasteur: Young scientist*. Mahwah, NJ: Troll.
Scholastic Children's Dictionary. (1996). New York: Scholastic.
Spier, P. (1986). *Dreams*. New York: Doubleday and Co.

Other Books by David Milgrim

Why Benny barks. (1994). New York: Random House.
Dog Brain. (1996). New York: Viking Books.
Here in space. (1997). Mahwah, NJ: Troll.

Related Children's Books

Macaulay, D. (1990). *Black and white*. Boston: Houghton Mifflin.
Numeroff, L. (1985). *If you give a mouse a cookie*. New York: Scholastic.
Numeroff, L. (1991). *If you give a moose a muffin*. New York: Scholastic.
Numeroff, L. (1995). *Chimps don't wear glasses*. New York: Scholastic.
Numeroff, L. (1995). *Dogs don't wear sneakers*. New York: Scholastic.

CHECK AND CHART WEIRD AND REAL WEATHER WITH *CLOUDY WITH A CHANCE OF MEATBALLS*
(by Judi Barrett, ill. by Ron Barrett)

There can be too much of a good thing. In Chewandswallow people didn't have to buy or grow food—their diet rained down from the sky. Suddenly, though, things turned sour. One day there was only broccoli, all over-cooked, and eventually huge foodstorms forced evacuation (achieved on oversized peanut butter and jelly sandwich rafts). Teachers and children ate this one up, relishing the happily busy pictures and the imaginative foodtrips it engendered.

Children's Choices for 1979. Reprinted from *The Reading Teacher*, October 1979.

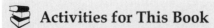 **Activities for This Book**

Reading aloud	Cloud study
Vocabulary and comprehension	Food study and a community
Weather reports	service project
Weather forecasts	Critical thinking
Journals	Sharing with grandparents

During his unit on weather, Tom Palumbo, an elementary teacher of a multiage–multigrade, lower elementary classroom, relies on the book *Cloudy With a Chance of Meatballs* as a stem for many weather–related activities. Tom considers himself a facilitator for the children's learning. He sets up situations for reading, discussing, observing, recording, and creating through writing and art. The children learn through the experiences their teacher structures. He begins his unit each year by reading this funny tale and comments, "The weather in Chewandswallow, however wacky, is a great way to get students thinking about weather prediction, forecasts each day, and even nutrition!" He brings out a weather indicator (see Figure 3.5) and tells the class that they will point the arrow to the kind of weather they are having.

Reading Aloud

After reading the story with his students, Tom has the children pretend to be weather reporters for the town of Chewandswallow. He has them write a weather report using several sources of information, including the book, the local newspaper, and the class weather indicator, and he gives them the opportunity to exaggerate and fictionalize the weather in their reports. The students then illustrate their reports with pictures they draw or cut from magazines. Tom compiles the weather reports into a class book titled *Weird Weather*. Tom also has his students pretend to be meteorologists and use their reports to give weather forecasts. He videotapes each of the forecasts so they can see and hear themselves later. Tom reports, "The kids really get a kick out of watching themselves give wacky weather forecasts. We often send the videos to our pen pals from another school district."

Figure 3.5
Weather Indicator

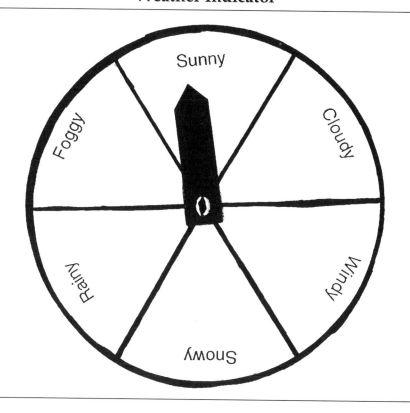

Vocabulary and Comprehension

Tom's students enjoy *Cloudy With a Chance of Meatballs* so much that they ask him to read it over and over. Their familiarity with the book enables him to work extensively on vocabulary and comprehension skills in large– and small–group settings. When choosing vocabulary words from a book, he looks for words that are essential to the theme and that will help his students expand their word knowledge. He focuses on the following vocabulary words: *brief, hurricane, shifted, drizzle, abandon, fog, prediction, violent, survival, tornado, stale,* and *sanitation.* He lists them on the board, pronounces them, and asks the students for the meaning. Then he rereads the book and asks students to listen for the words again. Sometimes students write the words on cards and categorize them in an open– or closed–word sort (Vacca, Vacca, & Gove, 2000). In an open-ended sort, students group words in any way they want; in a closed-word sort, they group words in a specific way; for example, by names or actions. Tom learns much about their word knowledge from the way they categorize according to parts of speech, number of syllables, words that are always weather words, and words with other uses. Tom may also ask students to categorize words in one of these ways.

He has a prepared list of questions to get students to think literally, critically, and creatively about the story (see Figure 3.6). Although he does not want the book discussion to become a question–and–answer session, he finds that questions stimulate thinking by helping students talk about the book.

Weather Activities

After the class has written fictionalized weather reports for *Weird Weather*, they turn to a serious study of weather. Tom brings in weather forecasts from a local newspaper to share with his students each day. He has the children talk about the weather predictions, and they discuss whether the forecasts were accurate. He helps the students set up a weather station in the classroom with a thermometer, barometer, and wind–direction indicator. The class keeps a weather journal and graphs each day's weather. Tom makes a large graph that records the daily weather for the month while the children keep individual charts. As a special event during the unit, Tom invites a local weather forecaster to visit his class. Students really enjoy learning about her job and realize that meteorology is a field that women enter also.

Tom introduces different types of clouds: cumulus, cirrus, and stratus. He takes the children outside to observe how clouds move and change in size, shape, and color. Each day the class observes and records the shapes they see in the clouds and the different types of clouds. They read *It Looked Like Spilt Milk* by Charles Shaw, which shows how children have envisioned clouds. Using cotton balls, the students shape the various clouds on construction paper.

Figure 3.6
Questions to Stimulate Thinking and Discussion

Cloudy With a Chance of Meatballs
by Judi Barrett

1. What was the most interesting thing that happened in the town of Chewandswallow? Would you like to live in Chewandswallow? Why or why not?

2. What are the advantages of food falling from the sky? What are some potential problems? Why would picky eaters have trouble living in Chewandswallow?

3. Which occupations would need the greatest number of employees in Chewandswallow (sanitation workers, house painters, carpenters, dry cleaners)? Which occupations would not be needed?

4. The author says that after the Sanitation Department fed the animals, they put the rest of the food into the earth so that the soil would be richer. What would that mean? How do people today help make the soil richer?

5. She shows the children the picture in the book with the newspaper headline, "Spaghetti Ties Up Town!" She asks the children to describe how spaghetti can tie up a town. What kind of weather can tie up a town in real life? At the top of the same page, the story reads, "the weather took a turn for the worse." She asks the students to explain the meaning of this statement.

6. Why did the people abandon the town of Chewandswallow? How did they leave? What changes did the move make in their lives? Would you have left Chewandswallow? Why or why not?

7. What real events might cause houses to be damaged, schools to be closed, or towns to be abandoned?

8. What did Henry and his sister think the snow and the sun looked like the morning after Grandpa's story? What are some other things you see every day that look like food?

Combining Food Study With a Community Service Project

Because there is a large emphasis on food in the story, Tom also introduces the topics of nutrition and food shortage. He discusses the fact that not everyone has enough food to eat, tying it into a community service project by having the children collect food to donate. He reports, "One year we donated our food collections to families who had lost their homes because of a hurricane; it couldn't have tied in any better!" The students write letters to their parents asking if they can bring a can of food to school to donate. They ask a community agency for names of people in their school neighborhood to whom they can give the food they have collected. Often they ask for a reference to elderly persons in their community and create greeting cards to send with the food. The project is a rewarding experience for all involved. Some of the food recipients even become adopted grandparents for other class activities.

As an added food connection and practice with the basic food groups, Tom asks the students to recall the different foods the weather brought to Chewandswallow. The class brainstorms a list. In cooperative groups, the children attempt to sort the foods into the corresponding food groups. Tom has the children draw and cut out pictures of the foods. Together they make a bulletin board with the food from Chewandswallow under the proper food–group headings.

Critical Thinking

Tom asks the children to imagine they work for the Sanitation Department of Chewandswallow. Their job is to get rid of all the leftover food after each stormy meal. He has the children imagine they have fed all the animals on the land and in the sea. They have put as much food as they can back into the soil, and they still have food left over. Teams of students are placed into cooperative groups called committees. Working in their committees, the students hold meetings to decide what should be done with the extra food. Each committee lists its ideas and presents them to the class. A master list is formed with all their ideas. Through a class group discussion and voting, the children choose the options they feel would best solve the problem. Furthering the discussion, Tom asks the students to think about all the problems cities can encounter when they are hit with various weather phenomena such as a snowstorm, hurricane, or tornado.

Sharing With Grandparents

As a culminating activity, Tom's class prepares and serves a pancake breakfast for their grandparents or adopted grandparents who are often senior citizens from the neighborhood. During the breakfast, the students read *Cloudy With A Chance of Meatballs* to their guests, reminding them that it is a story told by a grandfather to his grandchildren. Students then invite the grandparents to share stories with them about weather–related events they have experienced. Tom announces that there will be a Library Weather Center, a corner of the room where he has placed weather–related books for the month–long theme. Students are encouraged to browse through the books and read them during their free reading time.

Summary

Tom and his class have enjoyed a popular children's book with the prospect of other related books still to read (see page 46). He has integrated the language arts areas of listening, speaking, reading, and writing with science and critical thinking about current problems. He has extended the theme by having his class participate in a community service project and by having sharing time with grandparents.

Children's Books Cited

Barrett, J. (1978). *Cloudy with a chance of meatballs*. New York: Simon & Schuster.
Shaw, C. (1992). *It looked like spilt milk*. New York: HarperCollins.

Other Books by Judi Barrett

Animals should definitely not act like people. (1989). New York: Simon & Schuster.
Animals should definitely not wear clothing. (1990). New York: Simon & Schuster.

Old MacDonald had an apartment house. (1998). New York: Simon & Schuster.
Pickles to Pittsburgh. (1997). New York: Simon & Schuster.
The things that are most in the world. (1998). New York: Simon & Schuster.

Weather–Related Books

Allaby, M. (1999). *How the weather works: 100 ways parents and kids can share the secrets of the atmosphere.* New York: Reader's Digest.

Berger, M. (1999). *Can it rain cats and dogs? Questions and answers about weather.* New York: Scholastic.

Cole, J., & Degen, B. (1996). *Magic school bus: Inside a hurricane.* New York: Scholastic.

DePaola, T. (1984). *The cloud book.* New York: Holiday House.

DeWitt, L. (1993). *What will the weather be?* New York: HarperCollins.

Dussling, J., & Petach, H. (1998). *Pink snow and other weird weather.* New York: Putnam.

Ellyard, D. (Ed.). (1996). *Weather.* New York: Time Life.

Gibbons, G. (1996). *Weather words and what they mean.* New York: Holiday House.

Graf, M. (1998). *Lightning and thunderstorms.* New York: Simon & Schuster.

Hopping, L. (1994). *Wild weather: Tornadoes!* New York: Scholastic.

Hopkins, L. (1995). *Weather: Poems for all seasons.* New York: HarperCollins.

Hopping, L. (1995). *Wild weather: Hurricanes!* New York: Scholastic.

Hopping, L. (1998). *Wild weather: Blizzards!* New York: Scholastic.

Hopping, L. (1999). *Wild weather: Lightning!* New York: Scholastic.

Wallace, K. (1999). *Whatever the weather.* New York: DK Publishing.

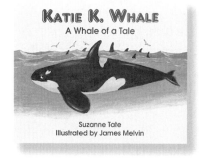

STUDY A WHALE OF A TALE WITH *KATIE K. WHALE*
(by Suzanne Tate, ill. by James Melvin)

Katie K. Whale's lonely adventure away from her podmates helps her to appreciate the warmth and friendship of others. Tate's delightful story not only teaches children about killer whales, but also helps them understand the importance of friends.

Children's Choices for 1997. Reprinted from *The Reading Teacher*, October 1997.

📖 Activities for This Book

Making a whale	Measurement
Studying initials	Fact versus fiction
Sequence of events	Writing an ending
Language patterns	Charting
Long $\bar{a}$ words	Rhyming and drama
Compare and contrast	

Four teachers of grades kindergarten, 1, 2, and 3 at a charter school in a coastal town worked together on a schoolwide theme: the ocean. They gathered children's books relating to oceans and sea life. One book in particular, *Katie K. Whale*, really caught the students' attention, so their teachers developed activities from this book, which crossed not only grades, but subjects as well.

Greeting Katie K. in Kindergarten

"*Katie K. Whale* was a hit from the first day it was read in kindergarten," says teacher Lynn Sylvia. "Children keep asking me to read it again and again!" Because students are so interested in the tale as well as the many facts in the story, Lynn has her class create a life–size whale 13 feet long to place on their wall. They stuff it and finger–paint it. Then they draw their own whales for which Lynn creates a "pod" on her wall near Katie K. The individually created whales were "the young whales who live in the pod," announces Kevin to a classmate. Naturally, they name the class whale Katie K. and dub her the class mascot. Students name their own whales and label them in the pod.

Taking advantage of Katie K.'s name, Lynn talks about abbreviations with her students. She asks them if they have middle names and what their middle initial would be. She explains that initials are one kind of abbreviation. She makes a class chart of their names and has students practice daily by calling each other by their first name and middle initial like Katie K.:

"Brad P., let's play soccer today," announces Kevin.

"Nikki T., do you have your library book?" asks Shareesa.

Soon other classes pick up on the novelty of calling each other by a first name plus middle initial, and the sounds of names with initials fill the school.

Extending the Story in Grade 1

In Grade 1, teacher Erin Sullivan has students create a class book adapted from the book *Brown Bear, Brown Bear What Do You See?* by Bill Martin Jr. The first book was titled *Katie K., Katie K.* Students added lines based on something Katie K. might have seen:

> Katie K., Katie K., What do you see?
>
> I see Sammy Shrimp looking at me.
>
> Sammy Shrimp, Sammy Shrimp, What do you see?
>
> I see Billy Blowfish looking at me.

In another activity Erin places important events from *Katie K. Whale* on sentence strips. She divides the class into groups and has them sequence parts of the story. She creates similar cards with the lines from the class version of Katie K., and the students sequence the language patterns.

Erin always looks for opportunities to teach or reinforce skill learning in context. *Katie K. Whale* is ideal for work on a long *a* sound. Erin and the class identify the many long *a* words in the book. Students make flashcards, pictures, and sentences with the following words: *whale, tale, wave, Tate, play, late, mate.*

Thinking Skills in Grade 2

In Grade 2, teacher Michelle Theberge places a large Venn diagram on a poster in front of the room and invites the class to brainstorm with her the similarities and differences between whales and fish. As she fills in the diagram, students fill in their personal copies (see Figure 3.7).

To practice measurement, Michelle's students cut out whales that are exactly one foot long. Students use the whales as measuring instruments to measure various items in their classroom:

Figure 3.7
Venn Diagram

Katie K. Whale
by Suzanne Tate

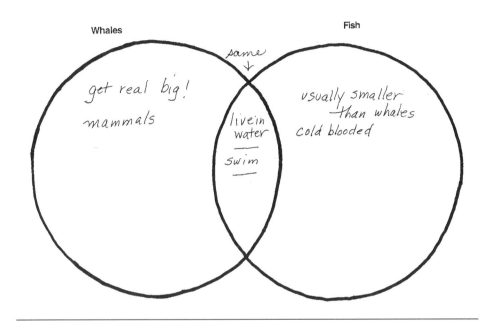

"The chalkboard eraser is one half of a whale long," announces Chris.

"My chalk is one fourth of a whale long," says Danielle.

"Let's decide how many inches are in a half and a quarter of your whales," Michelle reminds them.

Michelle uses multiple copies of the book in an activity in which students separate fact and fiction in the story. She divides the class into small groups and gives each group a copy of the book. They go through the story and generate lists of facts and fiction. Then they use the whale resource books (see related books at the end of this section) to check their facts and add additional ones. They also look for myths or beliefs that are untrue about whales to add to their Fact or Fiction Chart (see Figure 3.8, page 50).

Figure 3.8
Fact or Fiction Chart

Fact	Fiction
Killer whales are orcas orcas are black and white they "live" in pods	they don't really kill they don't talk like Katie K.

Creating in Grade 3

In Grade 3, teacher Brenda Wordell has learned that her students have many creative story endings. She stops the story at the point where Katie K. lags behind her pod. Her students write their own endings even before they know author Suzanne Tate's ending. Brenda tells the students they will send their endings to Suzanne Tate, along with letters telling her how much they loved Katie K.

Brenda works on map skills by having her students create a migration map for whales. After students have reviewed oceans and continents on a large world map, she gives students a blank outline of a world map. They work in groups to label the oceans and continents. Then they identify and chart possible migration patterns of whales.

Grade 3 students also create a class rhyme about Katie K. starting with the sentence, "There once was a whale named Katie K...." One student narrates while the others act it out. These performances are so entertaining that Brenda wants to share them with the other classes. As a culminating event, each class brings something to share with the other classes about their experiences with Katie K. during a "Whale Watcher" assembly for the whole school. Brenda states, "Sharing was a natural culmination for the excitement students had. It was also a valuable experience for students to see what other classes had developed from our common theme."

Summary

The four teachers chose the ocean as a relevant theme for their location, and narrowed it down to focus on whales. Each class did its own activities, coming together to share in a final assembly to which parents, relatives, and friends were invited. During subsequent parent–teacher conferences, parents were reminded to view the whale memorabilia throughout the classes and in the halls. Plans were soon underway for further reading and literacy activities related to whales and other sea creatures.

Children's Books Cited

Martin, B., Jr. (1983). *Brown Bear, Brown Bear, what do you see?* New York: Henry Holt.
Tate, S. (1995). *Katie K. Whale*. Nags Head, NC: Nags Head Art.

Other Books by Suzanne Tate

Crabby and Nabby: A tale of two blue crabs. (1995). Nags Head, NC: Nags Head Art.
Danny and Daisy: A tale of a dolphin duo. (1995). Nags Head, NC: Nags Head Art.
Ellie and Ollie Otter. (1995). Nags Head, NC: Nags Head Art.
Flossie Flounder. (1995). Nags Head, NC: Nags Head Art.
Pearlie Oyster. (1995). Nags Head, NC: Nags Head Art.
Salty Seagull. (1995). Nags Head, NC: Nags Head Art.
Tammy Turtle. (1995). Nags Head, NC: Nags Head Art.
Perky Pelican. (1996). Nags Head, NC: Nags Head Art.
Oopsie Otter. (1997). Nags Head, NC: Nags Head Art.
Great Sharky Shark. (1998). Nags Head, NC: Nags Head Art.

Related Children's Books on Whales

Arnold, C. (1994). *Killer whale*. New York: Morrow.
Berger, M. (1999). *Do whales have belly buttons? Questions and answers about whales and dolphins*. New York: Scholastic.
Gibbons, G. (1995). *Whales*. New York: Holiday House.
Kerrod, R., Webb, D., & Baker, J. (1998). *Nature watch whales and dolphins*. New York: Anness.
Kidd, N. (1992). *Whales, sharks, and other sea creatures*. Los Angeles: Lowell House.
Milton, J. (1993). *Whales and other creatures of the sea*. New York: Random House.
Moore, E. (2000). *Magic school bus wild whale watch*. New York: Scholastic.
Pfister, M., & James, J.A. (1998). *Rainbow fish and the big blue whale*. New York: North–South Books.
Posell, E.Z. (1990). *Whales and other sea mammals*. Danbury, CT: Grolier.

Raffi & Wolff, A. (1997). *Baby Beluga*. New York: Crown Books.

Schuch, S. (1999). *A symphony of whales*. San Diego, CA: Harcourt Brace.

Sheldon, D. (1997). *The whales' song*. New York: Viking–Penguin.

Simon, S. (1992). *Whales*. New York: HarperCollins.

Wythe, M. (1995). *The great whales*. New York: Putnam.

OPEN THE DOOR TO SHARING WITH *THE DOORBELL RANG* (by Pat Hutchins)

Each time Victoria and Sam sit down to eat Ma's cookies, the doorbell rings. It's always friends who want some of their cookies. With only one cookie left each, the doorbell rings again. They hesitantly answer the door and happily find Grandma with more cookies to share.

Children's Choices for 1987. Reprinted from *The Reading Teacher*, October 1987.

 Activities for This Book

Questions as prompts	Extend reading
Background knowledge	Books on sharing
Motivation to read	Number and concept books
Predict story from cover and title	Math experiences
Teacher read aloud	Charting
Choral reading	Measuring
Retell and drama	Graphing
Take the parts of characters	Oral language
Sequence story events	Masks and feelings

Nancy Lodge works with second-grade students in a suburban school setting. She chooses *The Doorbell Rang* because of its predictable text and cumulative story line. This book provides models of language and opportunities to talk about, understand, and construct story meanings, which are important activities for young readers (McGee, 1998). Nancy sees many applications she can make to the content area of math, which she believes can be more real to her students when illustrated in children's literature (Cohn & Wendt, 1992). She also sees opportunities to involve the children's families, which strengthens learning (Glazer & Burke, 1994). She thinks her students will relate to Sam's and Victoria's feelings of dismay as more and more of their friends arrive to share the plate of chocolate chip cookies. She believes the content of the story will build positive reading attitudes and a classroom environment conducive to literacy.

Introducing the Story

Nancy begins her lesson by ringing a doorbell that she obtained from a home supply store and mounted outside the classroom. She invites the children to explore their feelings as they hear the bell, by asking questions:

Who could be at the door when the doorbell rings in your house?

Are you happy to hear the doorbell ring?

How does your family feel when the doorbell rings? In my house, sometimes we don't feel like opening the door.

Let's guess: Who could be at the door when the bell rings at the house in our story?

Nancy further encourages students to talk about what they can predict from the title and cover of the book. She then calls her students' attention to the story and the plate of cookies the two children are about to eat, how many cookies each child might receive, and what problems will arise when the doorbell rings.

Will the cookies have to be shared with others?

Nancy reads the book to the children, making sure the pictures are easily seen by each of them. She encourages the students to comment on how Sam and Victoria are feeling as more and more visitors arrive, and to offer suggestions as to how the newcomers can be included in their snack. As the story progresses and phrases are repeated, Nancy encourages the students to read aloud with her the lines that are repeated from page to page:

"You can share the cookies."

"No one makes cookies like Grandma."

During a subsequent reading of the book, Nancy capitalizes on the students' enthusiasm by dividing the class and using a choral reading technique (Vacca, Vacca, & Gove, 2000). Half the students will read the predictable line, "'No one makes cookies like Grandma,' said Ma," and half will add the phrase, "as the doorbell rang," at the conclusion of each page.

Retelling and Dramatizing

The children want to hear the story again and again, so Nancy devises ways to vary it and to get students actively involved. She buys chocolate chip cookies and sprays them with a protective coating so that they can be used repeatedly for story–related activities. She warns the children that these cookies cannot be eaten, and to prove her point she invites the children to smell them. "See how funny they smell? Don't eat these, but some day we'll have some real chocolate chip cookies just like those in the story, OK?" The children eagerly agree, having loved the story and wanting more involvement with it.

Nancy pairs the students in the class and places 12 chocolate chip cookies on a plate. One pair of students, acting as Sam and Victoria, sits at a table and states that they will have six cookies each. The next pair of students rings the doorbell, which is answered by Nancy playing the role of the mother. The new pair sits at the table and the children divide the cookies into three for each. As the story progresses, the children divide their cookies to accommodate new arrivals who enter the house after ringing the doorbell. Finally, they are down to one cookie for each child at the table: 12 cookies for 12 children. They all sigh as the doorbell rings again. Surprise! It is actually a student's grandmother, who plays the part of the grandma in the story, who arrives with a big batch of chocolate chip cookies that the class will share.

After reading the story several times, Nancy has the children read lines from the story that she has put on sentence strips. The first reading is in random order with sentences appearing from anywhere in the book. Then copies of these sentences are handed out and pairs of students arrange the strips in the proper sequence according to the story. Both the sentence strips and several plates of "work cookies" are placed at learning centers that the children visit repeatedly in the days ahead to read and retell the story in pairs or small groups.

Extending Reading

Sharing emerges as a theme and Nancy reads several books on sharing that tie in with a writing activity. Nancy reads aloud during group time (which is called Story Circle) and talks about how important it is to be thoughtful and to share. She invites students to gather near her and help her read. Some students are able to read along chorally while others read along with a word or two. The class talks together as a precomposing activity that leads to a writing experience. The students write journal entries about an experience of sharing something special to them, or when they had an opportunity to share and did not. For those students reluctant to write, Nancy has them draw a picture of the incident. All students share their writing or pictures during group share time. Nancy recognizes differences in literacy development and affirms a child's "pen and paper" contact regardless of the level of literacy displayed.

Books on numbers and multiple concepts are also shared to build the children's exposure to numeracy. The concepts of one–to–one correspondence and graphic preparation for skip counting, such as counting by 2s or 3s, can be introduced with *The Doorbell Rang*, and reinforced through related titles. (See related books on page 59.)

Math Experiences

Although the division process is not a concept to teach in Grade 2, Nancy sees an easy way to lay the foundation. She has the children assist her in charting the relationship between the number of children that keep arriving and the number of cookies they get (see Figure 3.9, page 56).

Figure 3.9
Charting Children and Cookies

Number of children	Number of Cookies	Number of cookies each
2	12	6
2 + 2 = 4	12	3
2 + 2 + 2 = 6	12	2
2 + 2 + 2 + 6 = 12	12	1

Because the students are studying measurement in math class, Nancy decides to have the children measure and mix the ingredients for chocolate chip cookies. They arrange the dough on cookie sheets and count to be sure that there are enough cookies for each child in the class. Another adult bakes the cookies while Nancy continues her lesson. The children talk about sets, equal sets, and how many cookies each child would get if they made different amounts of cookies. As they review the story, the cookies finish baking. It is a wonderful learning experience for the children, not only to have the cookies for their snack time, but to decide how the remaining cookies should be shared. There are not enough cookies for each child in the class to receive more than one, but there are a few cookies left over. They discuss with whom the cookies should be shared: the cafeteria workers who let them use the oven, the maintenance workers who keep their classroom neat and clean, the mother who mixed and measured with them, the principal of the school, or after a gentle reminder, their teachers. In all their consideration of others, the students had forgotten about the teachers who helped them with the lesson. Not feeling slighted, Nancy turns this into a learning event, too: "It's easy to forget about sharing with those we see all the time," she suggests.

As the students enjoy their treats, discussions arise about favorite kinds of cookies. Nancy turns this into a teachable moment by having the children draw a bar graph of their favorite cookies (see Figure 3.10). Perhaps it was the power of the moment, but chocolate chip cookies were the overwhelming favorite.

**Figure 3.10
Graph of Favorite Cookies**

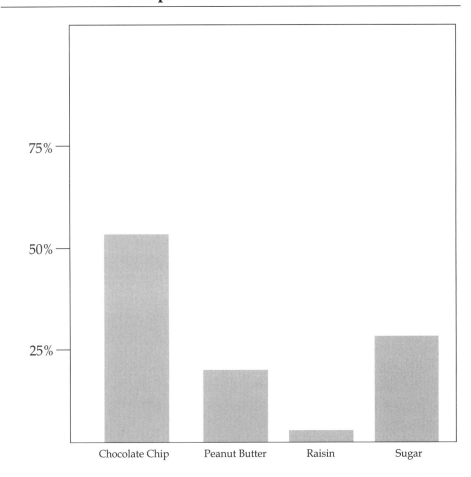

Oral Language

As a culminating activity, Nancy has the students study the illustration on the last page of *The Doorbell Rang*. The students pay particular attention to the expressions on the faces of the children as the doorbell rang when there are no more cookies to share. The students make paper–plate masks that show the different feelings they might have, then express their feelings while wearing the masks. It is very helpful for some of the children to have the mask; quiet students who rarely volunteer to share speak freely behind the mask.

Most children readily relate to a grandparent coming to the rescue, which opens the door, figuratively speaking, for new adventures with books dealing with extended family members and their roles in the children's lives. Therefore, what began as a delightful exposure to sharing and concepts about numbers continues to engage children in books about relationships and caring.

Summary

Nancy's students participated in literacy events through a story that had meaning in their lives. They engaged in predicting, reading chorally, dramatizing, and retelling the story through sequence cards and writing. Nancy extended their reading in two areas: sharing and math. She easily connected math concepts, involving the students in charting and graphing. She wove an oral language component throughout the lesson sequence, ending with a comfortable way to express feelings. Her children can eagerly pursue more books by Pat Hutchinson, as well as a variety of math counting and concept books and books on sharing.

Children's Book Cited

Hutchins, P. (1987). *The doorbell rang*. New York: Greenwillow.

Other Books by Pat Hutchins

Don't forget the bacon! (1995). New York: Scholastic.
Rosie's walk. (1987). New York: Scholastic.
The surprise party. (1991). New York: Aladdin.
The wind blew. (1993). New York: Scholastic.

Related Children's Books
Math Counting and Concepts

Aker, S. (1990). *What comes in 2's, 3's, & 4's?* New York: Simon & Schuster.
Crews, D. (1986). *Ten black dots*. New York: Greenwillow.
Hollander, C. (1994). *Ten toads and eleven lizards*. New York: McClanahan.
McGrath, B. (1998). *The Cheerios counting book*. New York: Scholastic.
McMillan, B. (1991). *Eating fractions*. New York: Scholastic.
O'Keefe, S. (1989). *One hungry monster*. New York: Scholastic.
Walsh, E. (1991). *Mouse count*. New York: Scholastic.
Wise, W. (1993). *Ten sly piranhas*. New York: Scholastic.

Sharing

Kadono, E. (1999). *Grandpa's soup*. Grand Rapids, MI: Wm. B. Eerdmans.
Moost, N. (1999). *It's all mine! – Or the little raven's mischief*. New York: Abbeville Press.
Munsch, R. (1999). *We share EVERYTHING!* New York: Scholastic.
Udry, J.M. (1971). *What Mary Jo shared*. New York: Scholastic.

EXPLODE INTO LITERACY WITH *THE MAGIC SCHOOL BUS BLOWS ITS TOP: A BOOK ABOUT VOLCANOES*
(by Joanna Cole, ill. by Bruce Degen)

Another book in the popular series, this story tells of Ms. Frizzle and her class trip to a volcano on an undiscovered island.

Children's Choices for 1997. Reprinted from *The Reading Teacher*, October 1997.

Activities for This Book

Use globe to discuss earth	Read to each other
Use Playdough to show volcanic movement	View video
Read aloud by teacher	Compare and contrast book and video
Directed Reading–Thinking Activity	Related reading and thinking
Write and illustrate in journals	K–W–L
Sharing	Art
Peer Pals	Create a volcano on paper
	Display volcano and journal

Rachel Westra, a teacher in a large urban public school system, engages her first– and second–grade students in one of the popular Magic School Bus series books, *The Magic School Bus Blows Its Top: A Book About Volcanoes.* As she reflects on her philosophy of teaching, her choices of children's literature, and her goals of instruction, Rachel annually checks the Children's Choices list because she wants to select books that she knows have a "proven track record" with children. She can use the list to provide books of interest within her students' age ranges and believes her students will gain confidence in their own reading ability by choosing books that are favorites of other children. She knows that confidence in reading ability, time to read, choice of what to read, and books that inspire and motivate children are key ingredients of her literacy program (Pressley, 1998). She believes that children learn to read by being exposed to good literature enthusiastically introduced by a teacher who integrates listening, speaking, reading, and writing in a series of lessons. She also realizes that an interest in books will have to be developed in many of her students.

Rachel's school population includes children from urban and suburban areas of the city, from families in which both parents work, and from single–parent families. Most of the children have limited experiences with books and literacy. Several speak English as a second language and have spent time in bilingual programs. Rachel has found that exposing them to books with a familiar story and talking about the story aids their literacy development (Battle, 1995). She finds that they are eager to communicate about stories.

Because the television is a prominent part of her students' lives, Rachel believes a book with a television connection would excite them. Rachel wants to connect with children's prior knowledge. Because she is certain the students are familiar with the Magic School Bus videos, even if they have not read the books, the book she has chosen will relate to their experiences by way of television, which she hopes will motivate them to read more.

Rachel considers many of her students to be at–risk learners because they lack home literacy experiences and a well-developed personal literacy (Spiegel, 1992). She knows they need to learn the power code of word–attack skills (the sound-symbol connection taught in phonics instruction). She later will use *The Magic School Bus Blows Its Top* as a source for word work and for teaching many literacy concepts, including skills lessons designed to teach the power code (Spiegel, 1992). First, however, she and the children will enjoy the book holistically (Goodman, 1986, 1996), which will set the context for later attention to specific skills.

Rachel also likes to make content area connections from children's literature. The science connection to volcanoes fits her school's curriculum, which includes a study of natural disasters and events. She likes to incorporate the visual arts because she thinks they have the power to "move the mind" as well as use some creative energy. She devises a simple project that she alone can carry out with the children, because she also provides art in the classroom. In addition, Rachel facilitates comprehension by using variations of the Directed Reading–Thinking Activity (DRTA) (Stauffer, 1975) and K–W–L (Ogle, 1986).

Introducing Volcanoes

With the students seated before her, Rachel holds up a globe of the world, leading students to talk about the world and its physical components. Using a ball of blue Playdough that she has carefully sliced, separated with wax paper, and reformed into a ball, Rachel shows how the earth's plates shift. She talks about how pressure builds and how magma is released and explodes, and the volcano blows its top. She directs the students' attention to a table where she has constructed a mountain of modeling clay around a jar that contains baking soda and a few drops of yellow and red food coloring. She tells them to watch as she pours vinegar into the jar.

"Wow!" exclaims Micah, "Is that a real volcano?"

"No," responds Rachel, "a real volcano is millions of times more powerful and very destructive. I wanted you to see how the magma comes out the top, just like my mixture bubbled out."

Reading About Volcanoes

Rachel reads aloud *The Magic School Bus Blows Its Top*, as she does when introducing all new books. She asks for students' predictions of what will occur, following a format similar to the DRTA. Students' predictions are written on a chart, reviewed periodically, and modified throughout the reading of the book:

"I think the bus will fall into the volcano," says Sharese.

"No, it won't," says Simone. "You know the Magic School Bus always comes back on TV with another trip some place."

"Let's write down both your predictions. Remember now, as I read, you're listening for proof that one of the predictions did or didn't happen," says Rachel.

She reads aloud, stopping now and then to check on the predictions. Sharese is disappointed that her prediction did not come true. Rachel assures her that simply making a prediction about reading is very important and makes us listen closely. She introduces the big words *verify* and *refute* to get the children thinking in literary terms that are beyond the true–false, right–wrong that they tend to associate with their predictions. After the reading and checking of predictions, it is time for writing.

Writing About Volcanoes

"Wow! A volcano book!" exclaims the class.

"Yes," Rachel agrees, "that's what it is. I'd like you to begin by drawing a picture of a volcano and writing a sentence about it (see Figure 3.11). We'll use this journal to write other things as we learn about

Figure 3.11

63

Illustration and Sentence About Volcanoes

CHAPTER 3

The Magic School Bus Blows Its Top: A Book About Volcanoes
by Joanna Cole

BRITTNEY BEACH

A VOLCANOE IS HOT

Ridgemoor Park

volcanoes. We'll also make more illustrations. I'd like to display your books when your parents come in for conferences. Then you can take them home and tell your families about our volcano study."

Sharing Journal Entries

As the students finish their journal entries, Rachel suggests that they begin sharing their journal entries with their "peer pals," the reading pairs that she has put together for this week. New peer pals are formed weekly. Some children have written several sentences; others have written a few words. Rachel notes the less prolific writers and will offer sentence starters in future journal-writing tasks to encourage students' writing development. Meanwhile, the class members have learned to accept whatever their peer shares without negatively reflecting the quality or quantity, and they have begun to practice offering positive suggestions to each other.

Viewing a Video

After students view the video *The Magic School Bus Blows Its Top*, they discuss similarities and differences between the book and the video. The video helps the book "come to life." Ms. Frizzle, the bus, and the characters act out the scenes and speak. Rachel encourages the class to consider how their impressions about the characters and events may have changed after seeing the video.

Related Reading and Thinking

Rachel calls the class to the front carpet, called the magic carpet because it is where the magic of books unfolds. She presents a K–W–L chart and asks the children what they know about volcanoes from the book and video. She helps them distinguish fact from fiction. She fills in the K column—What I Know?—and invites students to assist by writing in a word or letters. She then goes to the W column—What I Want to Know? The students are excited because the book has inspired their interest in volcanoes, and they suggest many topics they want to learn.

Rachel introduces one of several books about volcanoes she has obtained, *Volcano: The Eruption and Healing of Mount St. Helens* by Patricia Lauber, a Newbery honor book. She again gets out the globe to show the location of Mount St. Helens in Washington state. She tells the students that this is a book of fact about a real event. She shows them pictures throughout the book and reads selected sentences and picture captions. She then invites the children to suggest answers for the L column of the K–W–L chart—What I Learned. The children are excited, so Rachel goes on to list What I Still Want to Learn (see Figure 3.12). Because there are many things the students still want to know yet so little time in the curriculum, Rachel suggests one area they still want to know about as a topic for the month's writing project. She points to the volcano books

Figure 3.12
K-W-L Volcano Chart

K	W	L	
What I Know about volcanoes	What I Want to Know about volcanoes	What I Learned about volcanoes	What I Still Want to Learn about volcanoes
they're hot! they explode! even oceans can have volcanoes	Where are other volcanoes? How often do they blow up?	there's a big one in Washington. It's called Mt. St. Helens.	Where are more volcanoes? Do any keep on blowing up?

from the library that will be in their classroom library. Because of the differences in reading and writing ability across grades 1 and 2, she allows for some students to produce more drawing than writing.

Art Project for Volcanoes

Using art as a culminating activity seems to Rachel to be a fun way to end a series of lessons. More important, it seems to be a way to see evidence of children's learning about one aspect of volcanoes: their appearance. The project requires the following materials (see Figure 3.13): white paper, crayons, small pieces of colored paper, glue, and a small plastic cup. Each student will get a sheet of white paper and will color it to look like grass, dirt, or water in simulation of the area surrounding volcanoes that they have learned about in the books. Rachel explains that crayons do a more realistic job of depicting the scenery than the more popular markers.

After students have prepared their "ground cover," as they call it, they are given a small paper cup to glue upside down in the center. They glue small pieces of colored paper on the top, down the sides, and in a stream to indicate a lava or magma flow.

A classroom display will feature the volcanoes and the journals in which the students wrote. These will greet parents who come for parent-teacher conferences and who visit occasionally during the month.

Summary

Rachel has used principles of good literacy instruction to inspire her students' learning, to relate to their own backgrounds and prior experiences, and to integrate the language arts. She weaves listening, speaking, reading, and writing with each other and with the content areas of science and art. She extends the reading and writing connection beyond one book and one set of writing activities. She will observe the students' work and pick out areas of skills instruction to work on; but for now, she says, "Call this the affective part—we're getting into reading and writing that is within the students' capabilities and interests. We'll pick out the needs in skill areas next."

Figure 3.13
Volcano Art Project

67

CHAPTER 3

My Volcano   by _____

Color land all around volcano:
you can use brown for dirt,
green for grass and plants,
gray for rocks, and anything else you've seen
in nature.

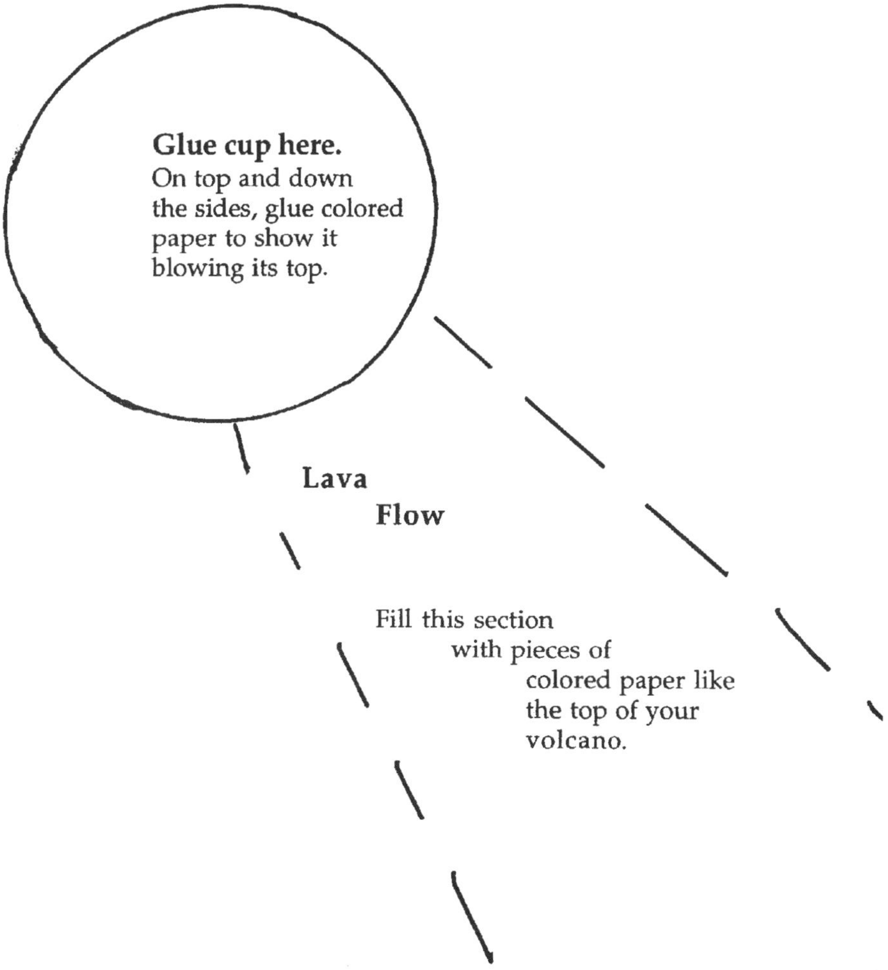

Glue cup here.
On top and down
the sides, glue colored
paper to show it
blowing its top.

Lava
Flow

Fill this section
    with pieces of
        colored paper like
        the top of your
        volcano.

Children's Books Cited

Cole, J. (1996). *The magic school bus blows its top: A book about volcanoes.* New York: Scholastic.

Lauber, P. (1987). *The eruption and healing of Mount St. Helens.* New York: Bradbury Press.

Related Books About Volcanoes

Arnold, E. (1997). *Volcanoes! Mountains of fire.* New York: Random House.

Bisel, S.C. (1991). *The secrets of Vesuvius.* New York: Madison Press.

Griffey, H. (1998). *Eyewitness reader: Volcanoes and other natural disasters.* London: Dorling Kindersley.

Kean, J. (Ed.). (1998). *Volcanoes.* Chicago: World Book.

Lauber, P. (1985). *Volcanoes and earthquakes.* New York: Scholastic.

Lauber, P. (1993). *Volcano: The eruption and healing of Mt. St. Helens.* New York: Simon & Schuster.

Nirgiotis, N. (1996). *Volcanoes: Mountains that blow their tops.* New York: Scholastic.

Stidworthy, J. (1996). *Earthquakes and volcanoes. Science Nature Guides Series: Changing world.* San Diego, CA: Thunderbay Press.

Magic School Bus Series

The magic school bus: Explores the senses. (1999). New York: Scholastic.

The magic school bus: In the time of the dinosaurs. (1994). New York: Scholastic.

The magic school bus: Inside a beehive. (1998). New York: Scholastic.

The magic school bus: Inside the Earth. (1989). New York: Scholastic.

The magic school bus: Inside the human body. (1990). New York: Scholastic.

The magic school bus: Kicks up a storm. (2000). New York: Scholastic.

The magic school bus: Lost in the solar system. (1990). New York: Scholastic.

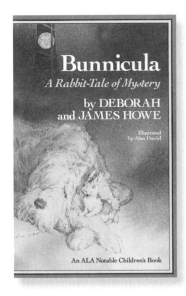

SERVE AS A SLEUTH WITH *BUNNICULA*

(by Deborah and James Howe, ill. by Alan Daniel)

Harold, the family dog, narrates this hilarious tale of a bunny who was found by the Monroe family in a Dracula movie. The well–read pet cat, Chester, observes strange nighttime behavior by the bunny. Humorous adventures result as Chester and Harold attempt to "save" the family from a suspected vampire.

Children's Choices for 1980. Reprinted from *The Reading Teacher*, October 1980.

 Activities for This Book

Predict story from title and cover	Drama
Teacher read aloud	Math
Silent reading	Graphing
Discussion	Reasoning
Response journal	Science
Write story in play format	Care of pets
Compose a sequel	Vegetables
Homonyms	Music and Art
Attribute web	

Aleigh Phillips introduces her second and third graders in a suburban private school to a delightful mystery story, *Bunnicula*. Most of her students are avid readers and read above grade level. However, as she plans her lessons, she tries to facilitate the reading of the book for all the students, even those who are not at the reading level of the others. She believes the Directed Reading Activity format, often associated with basal reading lessons (Vacca, Vacca, & Gove, 2000), will enable her to meet all the students' needs: introducing vocabulary, setting a purpose for reading, motivating the students, and guiding their comprehension on various levels through questions and activities. Aleigh is an avid believer in making plenty of reading–writing connections, which she attempts to do daily with her class. She makes some content area connections to math and science. She also gets the children involved in creating a play, along with music and art, about the book. She believes that art, music, and drama create the personal interactions that she hopes to develop (Gaines, 1992; Sebesta, 1987, 1992; Sinatra, 1994).

Bunnicula is told by Harold, the family's pet dog, who is convinced that a new family pet, a rabbit, is a vampire. The family derived the rabbit's name from a combination of "bunni" for bunny and "cula" for Dracula, after seeing a movie in which a bunny is found in a box with a note tied to it. This wonderful mystery provides a view of the world that is full of mischief, trouble, and cleverness. As the clues increase, readers keep asking themselves if Bunnicula is just an innocent bunny or the vampire Harold and Chester believe he is. Aleigh sees the book as an opportunity to connect with the children's love of fantasy and pets and their excitement with mysteries.

Introducing the Book

Aleigh introduces the students to the book by telling them the title and having them make predictions about the story from the illustration on the cover. Many ideas are forthcoming because of the print and the mention of the word *mystery*. On the cover, the title is in bright red, shiny letters, and the bunny has red eyes. Most of the children are convinced that the cat and the dog are plotting bodily harm to the rabbit, who is pictured much smaller than the other pets. After discussing the rabbit's unusual name, Aleigh assures the children that they might have other ideas as they find out more about Bunnicula.

Reading Aloud

Over the following week, Aleigh reads the book aloud to the class. She points out the main events in each chapter and discusses how they build suspense and cause the reader to wonder what the "real" story is. Chapter 7 is then read silently by the students. Although this book may be challenging for some of her class, Aleigh believes that by reading aloud the first chapters and by frequently discussing the book, she has prepared the students to handle reading on their own. She observes her less able readers for signs of struggle as the whole class reads silently. Before they begin Chapter 8, the students list information about Bunnicula they have gathered from the book thus far. They chart clues on a large poster with page numbers that cite the evidence (see Figure 3.14). Only then do the students move on to Chapter 8, the final chapter, thinking that they are going to solve the mystery of Bunnicula once and for all.

Figure 3.14
Bunnicula Poster

Question: Is Bunnicula a vampire rabbit? Answer the questions and give evidence.	
YES - evidence	**NO - evidence**
Chester sees the rabbit smile, and it has 2 little pointed fangs. p. 23. The tomato is white and has no juice. It has marks on the skin. pp. 33-36. The family found Bunnicula at the movie, "Dracula". p. 45 More vegetables turn white. p. 54.	Chester doesn't see any more strange behavior. p. 26. Harold hasn't noticed anything funny about the rabbit. p. 45. But the boys think it's caused by blight. p. 54. No more vegetables turn white. p. 67

Writing Activities

Aleigh uses reader–response journals that allow the children to re-act to the story as it progresses. She finds that a focus for their writing provides ideas and prevents writer's block. She suggests that each student begin the day's writing with a personal statement about whether or not Bunnicula is a vampire:

I think Bunnicula is, or is not, a vampire because _____.

Students are expected to add several sentences to their original statement, but this will vary among students according to their literacy development.

Aleigh encourages the children to support their opinions with incidents from the text, while assuring them that anything is possible in a fantasy story. Aleigh has a generic list of statements from which she also draws to set a daily focus. She phrases many of them as sentence starters:

When I read about _____, I felt _____.

I think that _____ will _____ because_____.

I hope that _____.

I wish that_____.

If I were _____, I would _____.

With each response students are asked to support their answers with more explanation and, when appropriate, evidence from the book.

Because the children are so enthralled with the story, Aleigh invites them to turn the story into a play that they can present to other classes in the school. She also points out that through this entire story they never knew what Bunnicula thought of all that was going on. She suggests adding Bunnicula's thoughts to the play they are writing. She groups the class so that each group is responsible for creating a page of dialogue for a chapter. While eight groups are each writing a page of the play from a different chapter, another group is writing a follow–up chapter. It is their responsibility to either solve the mystery or to write a sequel in which they solve the mystery. This group will read their chapter to the audience after the play is performed. Aleigh finds that because the children love the book they are able to complete these activities in creative ways. Undoubtedly because of the age of the children, Bunnicula is made to be a certified vampire in the chapter the group creates. Bunnicula continues to cause much distress to Harold and Chester.

Another writing experience the children enjoy is working with homonyms, which is an opportunity to cover skills listed in the schools' grade level curriculum guide. Chester, the cat, confuses *steak* with *stake*. He has a vague notion about pounding a stake into a vampire. He hears Mother asking Toby to put out a *steak* for dinner and thinks this is the *stake* he needs. Needless to say, a humorous scene develops as Chester tries to put the steak on the bunny. Using Chester's decision to attack Bunnicula with a *steak* to determine whether or not he is a vampire, the children explore similar homonyms. Aleigh finds a natural reading–writing connection with Fred Gwynne's books, such as *A Chocolate Moose for Dinner* and *The King Who Rained* (see booklist at the end of chapter), which engage children in the use of homonyms and provide a springboard for students to create their own versions of word pairs. Working with a partner they write and illustrate their words to be displayed on the classroom bulletin board. Aleigh further invites the students to come up with their own homonym lists, and she offers a prize at the end of the week for those who have the longest lists. Students are told that they may ask anyone about homonyms; they may write down those they learned and saw in class; they may take the lists home and ask their parents. On a Friday afternoon, an independent judge, the school media specialist, will examine the lists and declare a winner. Students are excited about contests and especially the prizes: homonym books by Fred Gwynne. Whenever possible Aleigh tries to teach concepts, such as homonyms, in the context of actual reading and writing. She believes that by encountering homonyms and making their own lists, students will learn more and be more enthusiastic about their learning than by filling in skill sheets.

After explaining the contest and allowing the students to begin their lists, Aleigh invites the students to begin another vocabulary activity by analyzing the three pet characters. Working within their same groups, the students fill in an Attribute Web (see Figure 3.15, page 74). In this activi-

Figure 3.15
Attribute Web for the Pets

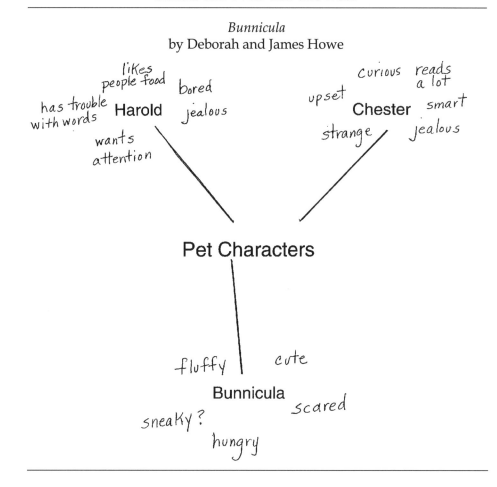

Bunnicula
by Deborah and James Howe

Pet Characters

Bunnicula

ty the students write the characters—Chester, Harold, and Bunnicula—on paper and then web characteristics around the names. Students are able to understand the characters in more depth, and to see relationships among characters when they discuss the webs.

Drama

Using the play they wrote, the children prepare to give their performance. Everyone has a job: issuing invitations, designing simple scenery, making paper–plate masks for costumes, and playing the roles. Each group of students performs their own chapter in a Readers Theatre fashion, in which they read the parts and use minimal props. Aleigh practices with the children until they are ready to take center stage. Several groups have taken Aleigh's suggestion about voicing Bunnicula's feelings, and the class has appointed a Bunnicula character to interject thoughts and feelings. The other classes love the performance, especially Bunnicula's interjections. The high point of the show comes when the children declare loud and clear that all the evidence points to the fact that Bunnicula IS a vampire.

Math

As they read the book, Aleigh takes advantage of the differing points of view about whether Bunnicula is a vampire and has the students cast votes and graph the results (see Figure 3.16, page 76). She does this after each chapter, producing new graphs each time. The class discusses the findings and makes comparisons based on the graphed information. Once again it is not surprising that most of the class feels that Bunnicula is a vampire. As the discussion continues, more students begin to express opinions that Harold and Chester were exaggerating and making it appear that Bunnicula was responsible for all the mischief and trouble.

Through a math connection Aleigh leads the students into reasoning and critical thinking when she repeatedly asks,

What do you think?

Why do you think so?

Can you explain your reasoning?

Can you support your thinking by citing evidence from the text?

Science

Children are encouraged to discuss their pets. This is a topic that children especially enjoy. Those children who do not have pets may talk about a toy pet or a pet they would like to have. Children with similar

Figure 3.16
Bunnicula Graph

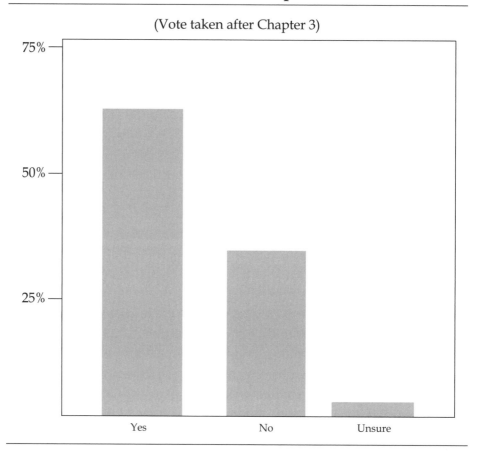

(Vote taken after Chapter 3)

pets or pet interests form groups and talk about characteristics, feeding, care the pet requires, and why that particular pet was chosen by the child or family. Students may share stories about their pets, which may become a new series of animal mysteries to be solved by future readers of *Bunnicula*. Pet stories can also become chapters in a class book to which each class member contributes a page.

Plants and vegetables, particularly those mentioned in the story, are another topic for a science lesson. The children happily talk about how they wish there were something in their homes that would cause vegetables to be unfit to serve. The prospect of never eating carrots had particular appeal, and in this story the students saw great possibilities for never having to eat another carrot. Not wanting the students to dwell on their dislike for vegetables but wanting them to develop more healthful eating habits, Aleigh invites parents to the classroom who bring favorite family vegetables prepared with personal touches they have added to increase their appeal. For instance, Jessica's mother brings carrots with cinnamon and sugar, which the children decide make carrots not so bad after all.

Music and Art

Several students in this class are gifted in music. Aleigh suggests that they work with her to make up a song or two to be sung in the play. Students enthusiastically create a rhythmic refrain to the tune of "Twinkle, Twinkle, Little Star" (see Figure 3.17), which they choose because it is familiar, and the line, "How I wonder what you are," alludes to the mystery of Bunnicula. The song includes clapping and swaying to the rhythm and serves as the grand finale to their performance.

To conclude the class adventure with *Bunnicula*, Aleigh has the children illustrate the different events in the story. She lists all the scenes on a chart and tells the children she will call their numbers. (In the beginning of the year, each child picked a number that became their "class number."

Figure 3.17
Bunnicula Song

To the tune of "Twinkle, Twinkle, Little Star"

"Chester, Harold, what is wrong?
Tell us while we sing this song!
Why this rabbit scares you so
   If he bit a tomato.
Even if he's Dracula
We still like Bunnicula!"

To be fair about choosing tasks, Aleigh could pick numbers out of a hat or invite a visitor to call random numbers when necessary.) This time the principal calls numbers between 1 and 26, the number of children in the class. The children step forward to choose a scene to illustrate. They work on their illustrations throughout the week and then the illustrations are laminated and compiled into a book for the classroom library.

Summary

Aleigh has capitalized on young children's love of fantasy with a popular book that taps into children's knowledge of and interest in pets. She facilitates their reading of a challenging book by reading much of it aloud to them. She weaves in a new concept (homonyms) in a meaningful way and makes a contest out of reinforcing students' new knowledge. She connects several writing activities, including the daily journals to which she adds a focus and sentence starters. Aleigh engages them in writing and performing a play and composing a song. She makes a connection to math through graphing and reasoning, and to science through a discussion about pet care and appreciating vegetables. She concludes with a simple art project. Aleigh's students are eager to read more Bunnicula adventures, as well as homonym books by Fred Gywnne.

The Bunnicula Series

Bunnicula: A rabbit tale of mystery. (1979). New York: Simon & Schuster.
Bunnicula escapes. (1994). New York: Morrow.
Bunnicula's frightfully fabulous factoids. (1999). New York: Simon & Schuster.
Bunnicula's long-lasting laugh-alouds. (1999). New York: Simon & Schuster.
Bunnicula's pleasantly perplexing puzzlers. (1998). New York: Simon & Schuster.
Bunnicula strikes again. (1999). New York: Simon & Schuster.
Bunnicula's wickedly wacky word games. (1998). New York: Simon & Schuster.
The celery stalks at midnight. (1984). New York: Morrow.
Howliday Inn. (1983). New York: Morrow.
Return to Howliday Inn. (1993). New York: Morrow.

Children's Books by Fred Gwynne

A chocolate moose for dinner. (1976). New York: Scholastic.
The king who rained. (1970). New York: Scholastic.
A little pigeon toad. (1988). New York: Scholastic.

HARRY ALLARD

JAMES MARSHALL

ESTABLISH A CLASSROOM COMMUNITY WITH *MISS NELSON IS MISSING*

(by Harry Allard, ill. by James Marshall)

The kids in room 207 are the worst behaved class in the whole school. One day sweet Miss Nelson does not come to school and is replaced by Miss Viola Swamp who means business. After the class is whipped into shape, Miss Nelson reappears, and all that is left of Miss Viola Swamp is an ugly black dress and a wig in Miss Nelson's closet. The odds–on favorite funny book of the year had the children exploding with laughter at the misbehavior in Room 207 and Miss Nelson's dramatic solution.

Children's Choices for 1978. Reprinted from *The Reading Teacher*, October 1978.

 Activities for This Book

Connect to prior experience	Figuring distance
Vocabulary	Science
Questions to stimulate thinking and discussion	Travel guides to the planets
	Social Studies
Create classroom rules	State study on the Internet
Classroom handbooks	Music, art, and drama
Journal ideas	Song about class rules
Poetry: An acrostic	Missing person posters
Math and Geography	Acting out feelings
Maps	

Kim Donovan, a second-grade teacher at a K–5 public school on the East Coast, uses the book *Miss Nelson Is Missing* during the first month of each school year. She uses the book as a device to bring awareness and attention to the importance of setting classroom rules and respecting the adult in charge. Further, she has developed many extension activities that her students enjoy, making the month-long involvement with Miss Nelson a worthwhile endeavor. She states that the book and activities are ones her classes never forget and that they refer to the book throughout the school year. *Miss Nelson Is Missing* provides Kim and her students fun cross-curricular activities that build enthusiasm for learning at the dawn of a new school year.

Kim begins by previewing and then reading *Miss Nelson Is Missing* to her students on the first day of school. Her first objective is to introduce the importance of classroom rules. She does a lot of reading aloud to the class and often uses a predict-read-prove sequence (Stauffer, 1975). She goes on to develop vocabulary, word-analysis skills, comprehension, reading-writing connections, content area connections and connections to music, art, and drama. Kim believes that children's literature can form the basis for much learning in the classroom.

Connecting to Prior Experience

Kim begins by discussing how students sometimes behave differently when there is a substitute teacher in the room. She talks to the students about occurrences that upset both substitute and regular classroom teachers. She asks, "Do students ever hurt teachers' feelings?" She follows with, "What might a teacher do that would be upsetting to students?"

Kim asks the students to make predictions about the story based on the title and cover. She asks the students questions:

Where do you think the story will take place?

What clues help you decide?

How is this classroom different from our own?

Who is Miss Nelson?

Why is she missing?

She records their predictions on a large sheet, which they review often throughout the story to check predictions, to support or refute them, and to add new ones.

Reading Aloud

Kim reads the story aloud several times over the course of a few days. She works on vocabulary and comprehension. She has chosen vocabulary words that are important to the story or that illustrate a skill she teaches (see Figure 3.18). Several words contain verb endings that she teaches as part of her curriculum. The students copy the vocabulary words on cards. They are asked to sort the words into names of people or things, action words, and describing words. Another time she asks them to group words with and without *-ed* endings and to separate compound words. In this way she introduces parts of speech (nouns, verbs, and adjectives), verb endings, and compound words.

Figure 3.18
Vocabulary Words

Miss Nelson Is Missing
by Harry Allard

rude spitballs gobbled terrible lovely refused detective police
hissed squirmed rapped whispered giggled homework

1. Write the words on cards.

2. Sort them into three groups:
   names of people or things
   action words
   describing words

3. Sort them by words with *-ed* endings and words without *-ed* endings.

4. Sort them by compound words (made of two words) and words that are not.

5. Sort the action words by the characters they refer to:
   the students, Miss Nelson, or Miss Swamp.

Discuss how the words were sorted and why.

Kim has developed a list of questions that stimulate thinking and discussion to ask throughout the story (see Figure 3.19). Rarely does she ask them all, but having written questions enables her to have prompts for discussion.

The questions include different levels of comprehension: literal, inferential, and applied.

Kim explains that some answers to questions are found in the words of the book, some answers need to be figured out, and some answers come from our heads. In this way she begins to acquaint students with Question-Answer Relationships (QARs) (Raphael, 1986), which are developed more in subsequent grades. For example, Kim asks, "How did the children in room 207 misbehave?"

"That's easy!" replies Sonny. "It's 'right there' because you read just what they did, like throwing paper airplanes and refusing to do their lessons."

Creating Classroom Rules

Kim has students draw, color, and cut out large pictures of Miss Nelson and Miss Viola Swamp. Then she provides cut–outs in the shape of conversation balloons. On the balloon shapes, the children each write a classroom rule that Miss Nelson or Miss Swamp has made in the story. Kim staples the rules around the pictures of Miss Nelson or Miss Swamp, adding the title "Their Classroom Rules."

Next, she invites the students to come up with rules for their own classroom. They brainstorm, and Kim lists their ideas on the board. They vote for five, which will become a poster, "Our Classroom Rules."

Writing Activities

Kim informs her students that schools often publish a handbook of school behavior. The class decides to publish its own handbook on class behavior. Students choose a behavior area to address: in the classroom, at recess, on the bus, or in art, music, and physical education. Some students write their own list of rules, while others do interactive writing (Button, Johnson, & Furgerson, 1996) paired with students from Grade 5.

Figure 3.19
Questions to Stimulate Thinking and Discussion

Miss Nelson Is Missing
by Harry Allard

1. How did the children in room 207 misbehave?
   What types of things did they do in the classroom?

2. Why were the children excited when they found out that Miss Nelson was absent?

3. Who took Miss Nelson's place as the teacher?

4. How did the children behave for the new teacher?

5. Why did the children listen to the new teacher?

6. What types of things did the children do with the new teacher?

7. After several days with Miss Swamp, how did the students feel?

8. What types of things did the children do to try to find Miss Nelson?

9. What did they think might have happened to her?

10. How did the children feel the day Miss Nelson returned?

11. Where was Miss Nelson?

12. Which events in this story could really happen?

13. How will Miss Nelson's students behave in the future?
    Have they really mended their ways? What makes you think so?

14. Suppose one of the students in room 207 misbehaved after Miss Nelson came back. What do you think the other students would do?

15. How would you describe Detective McSmogg?
    Do you think he will ever find Miss Swamp?

16. How did the children change in the story?
    What did they learn from Miss Swamp that they didn't from Miss Nelson?

17. What if your mother or father did the same thing Miss Nelson did?
    Would you like this change?

The fifth graders are trained to elicit as much writing from the second graders as possible and to assist them as necessary. Kim binds the articles in a class handbook, and students choose a class emblem for the cover. Kim reproduces enough booklets for everyone in the class to keep as a memento.

Meanwhile, journal writing is a daily activity. Kim gives the following choices to her students for their morning journal writing:

1. Write a letter that Miss Swamp might have written to a parent about a student's behavior.

2. Create a new ending for the story in words and pictures.

3. Choose a sentence and write about an event from the story. Sample topics may include

   The children in room 207 are terrible.

   The children in room 207 want Miss Nelson back.

   Miss Swamp is a strict teacher.

   Detective McSmogg is not very helpful.

   Miss Nelson has a secret.

4. Write a letter to Miss Nelson asking her to come back.

To encourage the students to write poetry, Kim invites them to create an acrostic name poem about Miss Nelson or Miss Swamp (see Figure 3.20). Students have already made acrostics with their own names, so they are familiar with the acrostic form. Because the levels of literacy competence differ among students, Kim expects different products, ranging from a picture with a sentence to a full page of writing. She divides the class into small groups and has a poetry sharing session as the students read their poems aloud. Three students are invited to read their poems to the principal at the start of each day until all have had such a prestigious appointment.

Math and Geography

Kim points out that authors often travel to different parts of their home country to promote their books. She has her students imagine

Figure 3.20
Acrostic Poetry

Miss Nelson Is Missing
by Harry Allard

N ice, but

E nough is enough!

L aughing,

S he is

O nly pretending to be missing.

N ow appearing as Miss Viola Swamp.

that Harry Allard is traveling from Salem, Massachusetts, where he works, to Boston, Massachusetts, to meet with illustrator James Marshall. She has the students locate the two cities on a map. She asks them to determine the direction Allard would travel. She then asks the students to pretend that Allard and Marshall are going to do interviews in San Francisco, Denver, New Orleans, and in the children's hometown. She challenges the students to trace the routes and then to figure the distances by using a chart of miles per inch on the map, again with help from their fifth-grade partners.

Science

In the book, one of Miss Nelson's students suggests that Miss Nelson might have gone to Mars. Kim decides to introduce *The Magic School Bus: Lost in the Solar System* to represent what a class trip through the solar system might be like.

After reading the story to the students and showing some informational books on outer space, Kim asks which planets they would most like to visit and why. Together they discuss the drawbacks of going there. With their fifth-grade partners, the students work in cooperative groups to create four-page travel guides to a planet, using informational books and Internet resources. Each travel guide includes the name of the planet, its special features, things to do there, and what supplies to take. The students illustrate a cover for their guides to show what their planet looks like.

Social Studies Using the Internet

On the cover of *Miss Nelson Is Missing*, there is a picture of a map of Texas and the Texas state flag. Kim explains to the children that the illustrator, James Marshall, grew up in Texas. She helps the students locate Texas on a map of the United States. During their time in the computer lab, Kim's class looks up Texas on the Internet to confirm the information on the cover and to find out the Texas state bird and flower. She has each student choose a different state and, with their fifth-grade partners, find its location, flag, bird, and flower. With their information, students create drawings, paintings, or mobiles of their states for a hall display, "Our United States."

Music, Art, and Drama

Kim works with her students and the music teacher to create a song about important rules for the classroom. They set the lyrics to the tune of "On Top of Old Smoky" (see Figure 3.21), and will perform it for grandparents on Grandparent's Day because they know grandparents went to school in stricter times and appreciate good behavior.

"And," added Karl, "our grandparents are old enough to know the song 'On Top of Old Smoky'!"

Kim also has the children design missing person posters for Miss Nelson. The posters contain a picture, a description of the teacher, what she was wearing when she disappeared, and other important facts.

Kim asks her students to act out some feelings represented in the story. She introduces the words by listing them on the chalkboard, asking the students to say them with her, and discussing their meaning in the book. She tells the students she has put the words on pieces of paper, which they will each pull out of a hat (see Figure 3.22).

As students pick a word from the hat that describes a feeling, they act it out, as the others guess the feeling from the master list on the board.

Figure 3.21
Classroom Rules

Sung to the tune of "On Top of Old Smoky"

Up here in our classroom

We gotta have rules

'Cause if we don't follow

We might be like mules.

So please do be quiet

When work's to be done.

And when we're all finished,

We'll go out for fun.

Figure 3.22
Describing Words

Miss Nelson Is Missing
by Harry Allard

noisy	curious
confused	obedient
mean	confident
sad	silly
upset	ugly
pleasant	unpleasant

Summary

By using the book *Miss Nelson Is Missing*, Kim's students are introduced to classroom rules and a variety of literacy and content area learning. Students enjoy hearing the story, referring to the characters, and participating in activities related to the book. Kim integrates the language arts with social studies, math, geography, science, music, art, and drama. She uses the book to help students take ownership for their classroom. After they create their classroom rules, Kim holds class meetings to address these rules when things do not run smoothly.

If students in Kim's class are unruly any time throughout the school year, Kim arranges for a visit from Miss Viola Swamp, using a black dress hanging in her closet at home. Kim says that the black dress from her closet does not come out too often. Instead, she often rewards her students for positive behavior. Their favorite reward is when Kim holds a funny-face contest followed by a paper-airplane contest, inspired by the students in Miss Nelson's class. Their second favorite reward is hearing more stories by Harry Allard.

Children's Books Cited

Allard, H. (1977). *Miss Nelson is missing*. New York: Scholastic.

Cole, J., & Degen, B. (1992). *The magic school bus: Lost in the solar system*. New York: Scholastic.

Other Books by Harry Allard

Bumps in the night. (1996). New York: Bantam Doubleday Dell.

Miss Nelson is back. (1986). Boston: Houghton Mifflin.

Miss Nelson has a field day. (1988). Boston: Houghton Mifflin.

The Stupids die. (1985). Boston: Houghton Mifflin.

The Stupids have a ball. (1984). Boston: Houghton Mifflin.

The Stupids step out. (1977). Boston: Houghton Mifflin.

The Stupids take off. (1993). Boston: Houghton Mifflin.

There's a party at Mona's tonight. (1997). New York: Dell.

Related Books on Planets, the Solar System, and Space

Bloch, C.Z. (1991). *Planets: Outer space sticker atlas*. Reisterstown, MD: Nickel Press.

Graham, I. (1991). *Our solar system*. New York: Scholastic.

Graham, I. (1991). *Looking at space*. New York: Scholastic.

Jackson, K. (1985). *Planets*. New York: Troll.

Books Used With
MIDDLE READERS

AMERICAN TALL TALES

A RIVER RAN WILD

THE HUMANE SOCIETIES:
A VOICE FOR THE ANIMALS

THE BOOK OF PIGERICKS

VASILISSA THE BEAUTIFUL:
A RUSSIAN FOLKTALE

YEH–SHEN: A CINDERELLA STORY FROM CHINA

CINDERELLA (FAY'S FAIRY TALES)

Books Used With Middle Readers

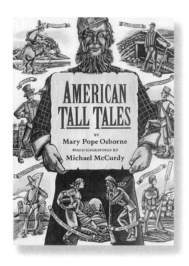

WRITE TALL WITH *AMERICAN TALL TALES*

(by Mary Pope Osborne, ill. by Michael McCurdy)

A superb collection of America's first folk heroes including Davy Crockett, Paul Bunyan, Sally Ann Thunder Ann Whirlwind Crockett, and 6 other unique characters! Sure to make you laugh. Historical notes give background about each character.

Children's Choices for 1992. Reprinted from *The Reading Teacher*, October 1992.

 Activities for This Book

K–W–L	Summaries
Fact or fiction	Brainstorm
Write a tall tale	The writing process: Four
Writing Book	paragraphs
Bouncers, Whoppers, and	Create a tall tale character
Taradiddles	Share with other classes

From Johnny Appleseed, "the ghost of the Ohio Valley" (p. 27), to Sally Ann Thunder Ann Whirlwind who informs Davy Crockett, "I can blow out the moonlight and sing a wolf to sleep" (p. 18), *American Tall Tales* captures the landscape and the characters of the American frontier. Mary Pope Osborne retells the tales in ways that maintain their integrity and yet are sensitive to today's concerns about exploitation of the environment and equality for all people, regardless of gender, race, or heritage.

Osborne captures the tales of heroes and heroines who

were like the land itself—gigantic, extravagant, restless, and flamboyant. Their exaggerated feats of courage and endurance helped the backwoodsman face the overwhelming task of developing such a land. (p. x)

Michael McCurdy's colorful woodcut engravings authentically depict the characters and the times.

Although there are many versions and titles of the various tall tales (see list on page 106), the popularity of Osborne's book shows a desire on the part of children and teachers to have several available at once. An added feature is the relevant history behind the tale that Osborne has included before she retells each tale.

American Tall Tales lends itself to comparison and contrast among the tales in this volume as well as tales separate from this book. Most notable for producing single children's titles is author Steven Kellogg (see list on page 106) who has produced several children's books featuring tall tale characters, such as Johnny Appleseed, Sally Ann Thunder Ann Whirlwind Crockett, and Mike Fink. Steven Kellogg's books have frequently been chosen by children as their favorite choices, and *Sally Ann Thunder Ann Whirlwind Crockett* made the Children's Choices list for 1996.

Kirsten Bolles teaches a split third/fourth-grade class at a small midwestern school. Although some of the curriculum is divided by grades, she has found that children in both grades love reading tall tales. They all like to distinguish between fact and fiction. Sometimes the distinction is difficult, which provides opportunity for discussion. Therefore, she has both the third and fourth grades join together in literacy around the theme Tall Tales. She goes beyond providing several versions of each tale and initiates an in–depth study of four tales, selecting two tales about men and two about women. Then her students create their own tall tales with a tall paper figure that they "dress" and decorate. Kirsten begins with the familiar tale of Johnny Appleseed and uses a K–W–L chart (Ogle, 1986). She then reads other tales and engages her students in the writing process to write their own tales.

Johnny Appleseed

"Let's see what you can tell me about Johnny Appleseed," invites Kirsten. Many hands go up, eager to share what they already know about Johnny Appleseed. "I know that he traveled many places and planted lots of apple trees," Lauren shares. "Okay," replies Kirsten, "Let's write that down on our K–W–L chart in the K column because that's something we know about Johnny." Kirsten continues to elicit a variety of responses while encouraging her students to think about what they would like to learn about Johnny Appleseed. "I wonder how many trees he planted," questions Jake. "That's a great one to write in our W column for things we want to know," answers Kirsten.

Following whole–group completion of the first two columns of the chart, the students read the Johnny Appleseed story in *American Tall Tales*. While reading this story, they complete the L column to share what they have learned about Johnny Appleseed. After they read Steven Kellogg's version and fill in additional information, it is apparent that they have learned a great deal of new information about this tall tale character. "Wow, I didn't know that he could wrestle with a grizzly bear and win," exclaims Holly. "Aw, he couldn't really beat a grizzly, could he?" inquires Jordan. This exchange gives Kirsten a great opportunity to begin a discussion about tall tale characters. The students share other examples of exaggerations.

Other Tall Tales

In preparation for writing their own tall tales, Kirsten shares a variety of tall tales with her students. During each story, they take turns pointing out exaggerations. "There's no way that Sally Ann Thunder

Ann Whirlwind Crockett could beat her older brothers in a foot race when she was that young," Brianne argues. Kirsten explains how the characters' special abilities help them get out of perilous situations. They examine Steven Kellogg's version of the tale for similarities and differences. Then they read about Mike Fink, another tall tale hero they can compare with Johnny Appleseed.

"I wonder if Johnny Appleseed and Mike Fink ever met," Kirsten prompts."I know of a riverboat named after Mike Fink!" exclaims Jordon. "Does it go on races on the water like Mike Fink's?"

After a discussion about Appleseed and Fink, Kirsten introduces *Swamp Angel*, a book with a strong female character like Sally Ann. She notes that it was a Caldecott honor book in 1995. She calls attention to the wood grained background and asks, "McCurdy uses wood engravings in *American Tall Tales* and Zelinsky uses a wood background for *Swamp Angel*. Why would two illustrators make use of wood in telling American frontier tales?" The students further connect to Johnny Appleseed and the importance of trees. "What about Paul Bunyan? He chopped them down!" exclaims Holly. "Yes," says Kirsten. "Trees were needed for food like apples but also to build homes. Trees played an important part in the development of North America."

The children, however, are more interested in the heroic feats of the tall tale characters.

Writing Tall Tales

After the students read the tall tales independently, they are bursting with ideas for their own tall tale characters. They complete a simple form that requires them to note exaggerations, special qualities, and problems that were overcome, which Kirsten combines with some ideas of her own to form summaries (see Figure 4.1, page 94). The summaries provide ideas to assist students in creating their own tall tale characters and examples of how each author used the character's special abilities to solve a problem. Kirsten puts the summary sheets, along with the other items, in a writing handbook to help guide the students through the writing process. Prior to choosing character names and other story components, the students also complete a "Bouncers, Whoppers, & Taradiddles"

Figure 4.1
Sample Summary

Book: Mike Fink
Author: Steven Kellogg
Tall Tale Character: Mike Fink

Special Abilities (Exaggerations):

- ran away from home at age 2
- joined a group of acrobatic frogs and traveled from pond to pond
- jumped on bed so hard went through bedroom roof
- jumped high enough that he could see rivers and boats in the west
- became a plow (crawled on knees) to help mom clear the land
- could shoot the shell off an egg
- hit a bulls-eye 3 times in a row in the exact same spot
- became a better wrestler by wrestling grizzly bears
- wrestled Captain Jack Carpenter for 2 weeks
- won every single wrestling match and got tons of red feathers
- lifted the front end of Blathersby's boat for awhile

Problems:

1. He wanted to be a keelboatman but Captain Jack Carpenter didn't want him on the boat. He challenged Mike to wrestle and said that if Mike won he would give him the red feather from his hat.

2. Hilton P. Blathersby had a big steamboat that was coming to the port. He wanted Mike's keelboat away from the dock. There wasn't enough room for both of them. He challenged Mike to fight for the river.

Solutions:

1. Mike wrestled him the first time and was thrown all the way to the Rocky Mountains. The second time he beat him and became the new captain of the boat and got the feather.

2. The two boats clashed together and Blathersby's boat sunk Mike's boat. But Blathersby's boat suddenly exploded. He survived, got in a lifeboat, and rowed toward Mike's floating hat to get the red feathers because now he was king of the river. Mike popped up out the water, wrestled him, and threw him all the way to grizzly bear country.

activity sheet (Schaffer, 1986/1987) (see Figure 4.2, page 96). This sheet gives the students practice in writing exaggerations they may use later in their stories. The students are given time to share the exaggerations they feel are their best. Excitement builds in the classroom as the creative ideas emerge. Jake relates to current weather conditions for his exaggeration, "It rained so hard that the drops made holes in the pavement!"

The students are encouraged to write down as much as they can on the sheet, Brainstorming Your Tall Tale Character (see Figure 4.3, page 97). Kirsten stresses that this part of the writing stage is to get as much information written down as possible. Although students will not need to use all the ideas found on the summaries, it will be helpful to have a variety of ideas from which to choose writing the rough draft. Kirsten checks each child's page for clarity and completeness.

Although a few students need a gentle reminder not to copy the stories they read previously, the majority of students have devised their own unique tales, taking ideas from their activity sheets and summaries.

The students are now prepared to write their rough drafts. Because this is the first story her third graders have written and it follows the tall tale genre, Kirsten has created a structured approach for this stage in the writing process (see Figure 4.4, page 98–101). The draft is divided into four paragraphs. Each paragraph has a prewriting section that asks questions that will form an outline of the paragraph. Kirsten reminds the students to look back at their brainstorming page to complete Paragraphs 2 and 3, which contain their character's special abilities and the problems being solved. After completing the questions, students write a rough draft of each paragraph by following the checklist at the bottom of the prewriting section. This ensures that their paragraphs are ordered logically. Upon completion of one paragraph, Kirsten meets with each child to edit his or her work. This individual attention allows her to read aloud the writing with the child, which will aid in the correction of grammar and sentence structure.

After approximately 2 weeks of the writing process, the students are ready to recopy their rough drafts onto a long strip of paper. They write the story in a paragraph format and are reminded to indent at the beginning of each paragraph.

Figure 4.2
Activity Sheet

Name _____ Skill: Creative writing

Bouncers, Whoppers, & Taradiddles

Have you ever told a bouncer, whopper, or taradiddle? They are all exaggerations that really stretch the truth! For example, do you remember the day it was so hot that all the corn fields started popping? Tall tales are full of these exaggerations. Make up some of your own bouncers, whoppers, and taradiddles by completing the following sentences.

1. I was so hungry that _____

2. It rained so hard that _____

3. She was so strong that _____

4. Its teeth were so sharp that _____

5. The _____ grew so quickly that _____

6. He ran so fast that _____

7. This baby was so tiny that _____

8. The wind was blowing so hard that _____

9. The animals in the zoo became so enraged that _____

10. We worked so hard at school today that _____

Challenge! Take one of your bouncers and expand it into a tall tale.

Figure 4.3
Brainstorming Your Tall Tale Character

Characters:

_____

_____

_____

Special Abilities/Talents (Exaggerations):

_____

_____

_____

_____

_____

_____

Problems/Events:

_____

_____

_____

_____

_____

_____

Solutions:

_____

_____

_____

_____

_____

_____

Figure 4.4
Prewriting/First Draft

Paragraph 1

What is the name of your character? _____

When was he/she born? _____

Decide where your story is going to take place.

_____

Tell a couple of facts about the character's family.

1. _____

2. _____

Tell about something amazing or unusual that happened to your character as a child. _____

_____

_____

How old is your character now? _____

As you write your first paragraph, darken in the boxes below to make sure you include each of your ideas. Go in the same order.

- ☐ The reader knows the name of my tall tale character.
- ☐ The reader knows when the character was born.
- ☐ The reader knows where the story is going to take place.
- ☐ The reader knows a couple of facts about the character's family.
- ☐ The reader knows something unusual from my character's childhood.
- ☐ The reader knows how old my character is now.

Paragraph 2

Look back at your brainstorming sheet and choose the first problem (or event) your character is going to face.

_____

_____

_____

_____

(continued)

Figure 4.4 *(continued)*
Prewriting/First Draft

99

CHAPTER 4

Describe a special ability or quality of your tall tale character.

_____

_____

_____

How will your character solve the problem using his or her special ability/quality?

_____

_____

_____

As you write your second paragraph, darken in the boxes below to make sure you have followed each step.

☐ I have started my paragraph with a good beginning line.
Example: One hot, sunny day…or It was a cold rainy night…

☐ I have described the problem (event) so the reader can picture it in his or her mind.

☐ I have described the solution using the character's special ability or quality.

Paragraph 3
Choose a different problem (event) your character is going to solve or face.

_____

_____

_____

_____

Describe another special ability or quality of your tall tale character.

_____

_____

_____

_____

(continued)

Figure 4.4 (*continued*)
Prewriting/First Draft

How will your character solve this problem using his or her special ability/quality?

_____

_____

_____

_____

As you write the third paragraph, darken in the boxes below to help you follow the order of your paragraph.

☐ My paragraph has an exciting beginning sentence similar to the one used in paragraph 2. Example: Then, one week later...

☐ The reader can picture the problem (event) in his or her mind.

☐ The reader can tell how the character solved the problem using his/her special ability or quality.

Paragraph 4

Is your tall tale character still living? _____

If not, when and how did he or she die? _____

_____

Each of the tall tales we have read gives some reasons why people will never forget the character. What are some things we will always remember about your character?

1. _____

_____

2. _____

_____

3. _____

_____

(*continued*)

Figure 4.4 *(continued)*
Prewriting/First Draft

101

CHAPTER 4

Checklist

As you write your last paragraph, darken in the following boxes as you do these steps.

☐ The reader knows if my character is living or when and how he/she died.

☐ The reader knows what people remember about my character. Example: People never forgot…or When people think of _____, they always remember that….

☐ My story has a good ending. I haven't left the reader wondering what happened.

Art Project for Tall Tales

Time to get out the wallpaper books, yarn, and sequins. Each student is given a piece of poster board on which to draw his or her tall tale character. "Don't forget to make your characters big," reminds Kirsten, "It will be much easier for you to dress and will look better with your story." The students have seen Great Grace, the tall tale character Kirsten created (see Figure 4.5, page 102). She wears a dress covered with wallpaper and has wonderful yarn braids with little blue barrettes attached. She is cut in half so the tall tale story can be attached between her upper half and lower half. The story is then folded in so it is hidden until she is opened up revealing a tall tale within a very tall character (see Figure 4.6, pages 103–105).

Holly searches diligently for the perfect pattern for her character's shirt. Lauren comes up with the unique idea of attaching candies to the front of her character's shirt to serve as buttons.

Kirsten wraps up the study and creation of tall tale characters by having her students visit grades 1 and 2 to share their tall tales. Their joy is evident as the authors eagerly read their tales and display their characters. More than once, Kirsten overhears the younger students say, "That's cool how your story is inside. I can't wait until I get in third grade and I get to write one of those." From the reading of tall tales to

Figure 4.5
Great Grace

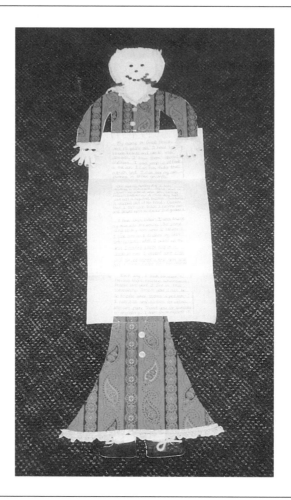

the completion of their own tall tales, Kirsten's students have gained a greater appreciation for this style of literature, for the writing process, and for coordination of text and character.

Summary

Kirsten illustrates the reading–writing connection at its best. With so many tall tales available in *American Tall Tales* and as individual titles,

Figure 4.6
Directions for Tall Tale Character Assemblage

Materials

- piece of paper 9" wide and 18" long
- copies of the attached paragraph sections (4 per kid)
- poster board (square or ½ sheet per kid)
- wallpaper books (optional)
- yarn, lace, and other art related materials for clothing (opt.)

Directions

1. The students will copy over their rough draft corrected paragraphs onto the new paragraph section you gave them. You may keep the middle two sections together. You could adapt this for younger kids by just having them do the two middle sections.

2. The students will then need poster board to make their tall tale character. They should draw in pencil first. Remind them that their character should be skinny and/or kind of long in the middle because when they cut it in half, the two parts must match. They should be very similar. See picture below.

(continued)

Figure 4.6 (*continued*)
Directions for Tall Tale Character Assemblage

3. The students can cut out their character. If you are letting them use wallpaper books, they should choose the pattern they want. Next, they will place their tall tale character on the backside of the wallpaper and trace around the section they wish to cover. They should leave extra wall paper on the bottom part of the top and the top part of the bottom section. See picture below. If students choose not to use wallpaper then they should just color it.

← extra wall paper
to fold in later

4. Wallpaper can be glued on as well as any other assorted art materials you may be providing.

5. The construction paper should be folded in three sections so the outer two touch when folded in. See drawing below.

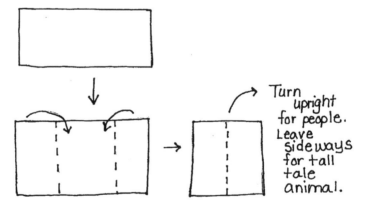

Turn upright for people. Leave sideways for tall tale animal.

6. The story can be pasted inside.

(*continued*)

7. When you are putting it together (I did it for them) the extra wallpaper will get folded over the construction paper flaps and stapled to the character. The middle of the character should match up when it is put together and look really long when the story is unfolded. If your students just colored it, then you will need to tape a little bit of paper to the back of their two parts and staple the extra paper flap to the construction paper. See picture below.

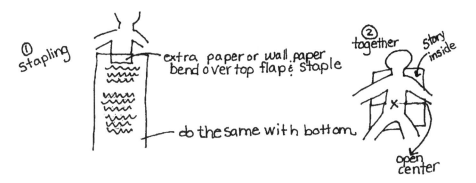

8. When you are all done, you can share these stories as a class or visit younger classes and share. My 3rd grade students loved that part almost as much as creating their characters.

Please feel free to contact me if you have any questions about this. Also feel free to use this as a base and go off on your own. I know you've all got great ideas of your own.

Bolles, K. (1998). Reprinted with permission

her supply of reading material is nearly unlimited. She finds a natural connection to a specific skill is her curriculum: distinguishing between fact and fiction. She uses the writing process and structures it in a way that all students can succeed. She provides the paragraph format for this first writing assignment of the year. The writing of students' own tall tales follows easily and is even more exciting when put into the shape of an actual character they can dress and decorate.

Children's Books Cited

Isaacs, A. (1994). *Swamp Angel*. (Ill. P. Zelinsky). New York: Penguin.

Kellogg, S. (1984). *Paul Bunyan*. New York: William Morrow.

Kellogg, S. (1992). *Mike Fink*. New York: William Morrow.

Kellogg, S. (1995). *Sally Ann Thunder Ann Whirlwind Crockett*. New York: William Morrow.

Kellogg, S. (1998). *Johnny Appleseed*. New York: William Morrow.

Osborne, M.P. (1991). *American tall tales* (Ill. M. McCurdy). New York: Scholastic.

More Children's Tall Tale Books

Blair, W. (1987). *Tall tale America: A legendary history of our humorous heroes*. Chicago: University of Chicago Press.

Cruzon, P. (1996). *Tall tales of the United States*. Baldwin Park, CA: Clear Creek.

Dewey, A. (1993). *The narrow escapes of Davy Crockett*. New York: Morrow.

Fleischman, S. (1997). *McBoom's wonderful one acre farm: 3 tall tales*. New York: Morrow.

Fowke, E. (1990). *Folklore of Canada*. New York: St. Martin's.

Garretson, J. (1997). *Johnny Kaw: The pioneer spirit of Kansas*. Manhattan, KS: Ravenstone.

Gleeson, G. (1997). *Pecos Bill*. New York: Simon & Schuster.

Kellogg, S. (1992). *Pecos Bill*. New York: Morrow.

Kellogg, S. (1998). *I was born about 10,000 years ago*. New York: Morrow.

McCaslin, N. (1996). *Paul Bunyan: Lumberjack*. Studio City, CA: Players Press.

San Souci, R. D. (1993). *Cut from the same cloth: American women of myth, legend, and tall tales*. New York: Putnam.

Schwartz, A. (1990). *Whoppers: Tall tales and other lies collection from American folklore*. New York: HarperCollins.

Steber, R. (1995). *Tall tales*. Prineville, OR: Bonanza.

West, T. (1998). *Teaching tall tales: Reproducible stories, writings mini lessons, geography, and map activities*. New York: Scholastic.

Thomassie, T., & Smith, C.B. (1998). *Feliciana Feydra LeRoux: A Cajun tall tale*. New York: Little, Brown.

Ullman, J.A. (1990). *Fried fog and other Cape Cod yarns*. Santa Barbara, CA: John Daniel & Company.

Young, R. (1989). *Ozark tall tales*. Little Rock, AR: August House.

Wood, A. (1996). *The Bunyan's*. New York: Scholastic.

DEVELOP SENSITIVITY TO ENVIRONMENTAL NEEDS WITH *A RIVER RAN WILD*
(by Lynne Cherry)

The Hash–a-way River was a clean sparkling river, an ideal home for Chief Weeawa's people. But "progress" changes all that. Then Oweana, a descendent of Weeawa, decides something must be done. A beautifully illustrated book to use for environmental units.

Children's Choices for 1993. Reprinted from *The Reading Teacher*, October, 1993.

 Activities for This Book

Theme and vocabulary	Experiments with water
Activation of background knowledge	Record in Water Journals
	Provide prompts
Vocabulary exploration	Write descriptive reflections
Teacher read aloud	Projects to reflect learning
Discussion of illustrations	From mountain top to river below
Recognition of philosophical differences	Diorama
Field trips	Research home water usage

Kathleen O'Neill was eager for her fourth–grade students to develop an awareness of environmental responsibility as well as to realize the impact that one person can have on effecting change. *A River Ran Wild* was a perfect choice on which to base her lessons. Kathleen believes science becomes real to children through the use of trade books and through actual experiences, and she advocates and supports the use of informational books in the classroom. Because Kathleen's students live in an area with an environmental education center and a water treatment plant, she sees opportunities to tie in to local concerns.

A River Ran Wild is a story of the Nashua River, which began about 6 centuries ago when a group of Native Americans discovered the crystal clear river and decided to settle near its shore. As time passed, settlers built villages near the river and dammed it for grist and sawmills, but still the river flowed free. Eventually, towns and factories emerged along with the Industrial Revolution in the United States. Chemicals, fiber, pulp, and dye were emptied into the river from factories until the Nashua River was ecologically dead. In 1962, Marion Stoddart organized the Nashua River Cleanup Committee to restore the river to its original state, which thanks to her efforts is now a reality.

Introducing Theme and Vocabulary

Kathleen prepares to read the book to the students by inviting them to explore the cover and make predictions about story content. The information from their sharing leads naturally into Kathleen's introduction of important vocabulary for the selection: *millponds, Industrial Revolution, pulp, dye, thatch, wilderness, current, downstream, politicians, dwellings, valley, invention, chemical,* and *pollution.*

Kathleen shows the students how to make a three–column vocabulary chart on their paper (see Figure 4.7), similar in theory to Routman's Have–a–Go sheets for spelling (Routman, 1991). The three columns are the vocabulary word (Word column), students' prediction about what the word means (Before column), and the definition of the word obtained from context (After column). Students guess what the vocabulary words mean and write their definitions in the column marked Before. Following the reading, they will fill in the After column.

Discussing Illustrations

As Kathleen reads the story aloud, she and the students discuss the primary illustrations and the small pictures that border most pages of the text. These illustrations are especially significant because each contains a story within the main story. The small pictures depict animals, objects, or buildings that show the changes leading up to and beyond

Figure 4.7

Figure 4.7
Vocabulary Chart

Text WORD	Prediction of meaning BEFORE Reading	Definition from Context AFTER Reading
Millponds	Something- like a Step from a tadpole to a frog	a place used to store water
Industrial Revolution	the Revolutionary War - a military place	time when new machines were being made
Pulp	the stuff in orange juice	something that comes from wood that is made into paper
Dye	like dying a shirt	Something that is used to change the color of something else
Thatch	a little door on a boat	to start building something, like a house
Wilderness	animals in the wild	forests - lots of trees and animals
Current	Something recent that happened - like in the news	water moving in a river
Downstream	like canoeing	place further along the river
Politicians	people that work with politics	people who work in government
Dwellings	dwell means to hang around	Places to live
Valley	like 2 hills + when you go down, that's the valley	land between mountains or hills
Invention	a new thing that nobody's ever thought of	new things made with new materials
Chemical	something that's in a drink or in food	bad things that pollute the river
Pollution	like people trashing the earth with cans + bags	waste that makes a place dirty, like the river

the Industrial Revolution. They also show what was important at different times during the history of the river. The primary illustrations portray the changing landscape as the saga of the Nashua River continues from about 1400 until the present.

Students are moved by the story, its simplicity, and its profound message. An emotional discussion ensues.

Jeremy asks, "How could the factories just dump their stuff into the river?"

"Perhaps they didn't know about the polluting effects it would have," suggests Kathleen.

"They must have known. Anyone knows what happens when you dump garbage in the water!" insists Lauren.

"Not necessarily," reminds Kathleen. "People didn't always realize the harm that could be done to rivers. They figured that whatever they would put in the rivers would just wash away." At this point the students revisit their Before vocabulary list and either verify the definitions they had previously stated or change them to reflect the material in the book, which they then list in the After column. Students volunteer answers for the Classroom Vocabulary Chart that they post in the hallway, hoping to interest other classes in the vocabulary and in the project they plan to do and share.

Field Trips and Experiments

To extend the students' knowledge, Kathleen arranges a visit to the Environmental Education Center of the Cuyahoga Valley National Park in Peninsula, Ohio. The center's program, "A River Runs Through It," includes the river, laboratories, and computers. The students not only gain first–hand experience with a river, but have the opportunity to interact with materials and equipment to promote an ecologically sound river. "They say a picture's worth a thousand words," comments Kathleen, "and the book's illustrations piqued the students' interest. However, actually going to the river and seeing such an impressive project will have a lasting impact on the children."

A second field trip is planned to visit the local water treatment plant to learn about the process and the machines used to clean water. However, before the students visit the filtration plant they engage in two experiments to build background knowledge: the first involves creating water pollution, and the second involves the cleaning process (see Figures 4.8a & b). Students feel reluctant to pollute the water, but are willing when they realize that they can try to clean it later. They also learn

Figure 4.8a
Water Pollution Experiment

Materials needed: A pan or pail of water.

Any debris that might be in a stream, such as nature's cast-offs, people's cast-offs, or pollutants from businesses or residences along a river.

1. Fill a dish pan or water table half way with water.

2. Gather materials that might end up in our rivers and streams such as leaves, sand, stones, grass, paper scraps, dirt, food coloring, and cooking oil.

3. In groups, use strainers, sieves, and cheesecloth to clean the water. (Provide containers to discard materials.)

4. Challenge students to work together to remove as many items and substances from the dirty water as possible. Have students observe and describe the methods that worked best. Have students list the items they removed and those they could not remove from the water. Discussion follows regarding which items were the easiest and which were the most difficult to get out of the water.

Figure 4.8b
What Cleans Our Water?

Materials needed

a.) A 2-liter plastic bottle cut in half:

Use top half which has been turned upside down as a funnel.

b.) Different filtering materials such as cotton, grating, small stones, sand, screening, and paper towels.

c.) Bottles of muddy water.

Groups will

a.) Decide which filtering material or materials to place in the funnel before pouring the muddy water through.

b.) Ask questions:

1. Does the water look cleaner?

2. What happens if you use a different filtering material?

3. What happens if you use more than one filtering material?

4. How could you make a better filter?

c.) Write questions and answers in Clean Water Journals to take along to the filtration plant.

that water is easier to pollute than to clean up. After the experiments, the students are prepared to visit the water filtration plant with an understanding of the process necessary to ensure safe water. They have recorded the results of their experiments in their water journals and have listed questions to ask the experts.

Descriptive Writing

Following their visit, the students eagerly discuss what they learned from the experts at the water filtration plant and share the results of their own experiments. They also share their additional questions.

Because they are bursting with thoughts, Kathleen has the students do reflective and descriptive writing. She encourages them to use prompts that she has provided:

Imagine a river. It is your river. Describe it—remember it is an imagined one.

How does your river go from the mountain to the ocean?

Describe what it passes along its journey.

How would your life change if you did not have water for one day?

Describe what a day without water would be like for you.

Change in the Land (Cronan, 1983), a book that inspired Lynne Cherry to write her book, explains the different philosophies of the Indians and the settlers toward the land, which Kathleen discusses:

From what you learned, how did the Indians and the settlers differ in their thinking about how to use and treat the land?

What were the results of each of these different philosophies?

Another book that influenced Lynne Cherry was *Restoring the Earth* (Berger, 1985), which documents 12 environmental success stories of individuals who have changed the world for the better. Kathleen continues,

What can you do to act more responsibly or to change the world for the better? Many students are making a difference. How can you be one of them?

Projects to Reflect Learning

Though Kathleen sees her projects as a conclusion to this unit of study, they are in reality only the beginning. Students pursue their particular areas of interest in completing one of three activities they share with the class. The first is to create a game called "From Source to Sea." The students draw a scene from a mountain at the top to the sea at the bottom on a large poster board. A game path winds its way from top to bottom. Spaces are filled in with bad and good ways that a river can be affected by people; for example, garbage dumped in river represents a bad influence versus removal of discarded items dumped in the river represents a good influence. Each space on the path contains directions to move forward or back a number of spaces, lose a turn, or take an extra turn. Students play the game with class members and roll dice to see how many spaces to move. The first person who obtains an exact number in order to reach the end is declared the winner. The students play the game with gusto.

Another activity that children may choose to do is a diorama, depicting the water cycle or the food web of a river. Several children create a diorama showing the effects of pollution and contrast those effects with responsible care of the environment. Other children choose to do research projects about conserving water in the home, which they do over the course of a month and report their findings to the class. They respond to the following:

1. Look at the last water bill from your home to see how much water was used last month.
2. Brainstorm ways to conserve water at home.
3. Try some of the ideas at home with your family's help.
4. Keep a journal of the ways you have conserved each day.
5. Compare the amount of water used on the next bill with the amount on the last bill.
6. Were you successful? Was your family able to conserve?

On a designated day, the children bring in their dioramas, the results of their research, and the game they designed for a wonderful culminating experience. Parents and grandparents are invited to come in to see the results of the children's study. Children offer all visitors a drink of pure water that is taken from a tap to which a water filter has been installed by the custodian. Children are interspersed throughout the projects to answer visitors' questions. On the following day, other classes visit with the same reception given to families. A surprise to the students is when the principal awards the class with the school's Good Environmental Citizens Award for their efforts to learn about and help the environment.

Summary

Kathleen has used a Children's Choices book to connect to science study and her own passion for preserving the environment. She integrates the language arts: speaking, listening, reading, and writing throughout the learning activities in which the children engage. She connects to local environmental facilities and gives the children hands–on experiments to perform on their own. She has the children maintain journals throughout the project to write and answer questions, to formulate more questions, and to keep notes of what they learn. She includes writing a descriptive reflection piece at the end. She provides options for their projects and an opportunity to share with multiple audiences. It is likely that she has developed a lifelong love of learning in these informed young citizens who will actively promote safe environmental practices in their community now and in the future.

Children's Book Cited

Cherry, L. (1992). *A river ran wild*. San Diego, CA: Harcourt Brace.

Other References

Berger, J.J. (1985). *Restoring the earth*. New York: Knopf.
Cronon, W. (1983). *Change in the land*. New York: Hill and Wang.

Related Books About the Environment

Nonfiction

Berger, M., & G. (1995). *Water, water, everywhere*. Nashville, TN: Ideals Children's Books.

Earth Works Group. (1990). *50 simple things kids can do to save the earth*. Kansas City, MO: Andrews & McMeel.

Elkington, J., Hailes, J., Hill, D., & Makower, J. (1990). *Going green*. New York: Penguin Group.

Haslam, A. (1996). *Rivers*. Chicago, World Book.

Markle, S. (1991). *The kids' earth handbook*. New York: Atheneum.

Miles, B. (1991). *Save the earth*. New York: Knopf.

Parker, J., & S. (1997). *Rivers*. Danbury, CT: Franklin Watts.

Sayre, A. (1996). *River and stream*. Brookfield, CT: Twenty–First Century Books.

Whiting, S. (1999). *Rivers*. Austin, TX: Raintree Steck–Vaughn.

Fiction

Baker, J. (1987). *Where the forest meets the sea*. New York: Greenwillow Books.

Baker, J. (1991). *Window*. New York: Greenwillow Books.

Dabcovich, L. (1980). *Follow the river*. New York: E.P. Dutton.

Dorros, A. (1991). *Follow the water from brook to ocean*. New York: HarperCollins.

Video

M.B.G. Learning Network. (1997). *Exploring rivers and streams*.

APPRECIATE ANIMALS WITH *THE HUMANE SOCIETIES: A VOICE FOR THE ANIMALS*

(by Shelley Swanson Sateren)

Each year 13 million of the 22 million dogs and cats born are turned over to animal shelters. This sad statistic shows why animal care should be a vital part of education today. The text mainly explains everyday occurrences at U.S. animal shelters.

Children's Choices for 1997. Reprinted from *The Reading Teacher*, October 1997.

Activities for This Book

Speaking and listening	Active involvement
Discussion/Brainstorming	Care of dogs
Our Responsibility Toward Animals	Write first–person story or letter
Guest presenter from the Humane Society	Diagram ideal animal facility
	Choose music for pets
Student research	Walk and play with pets
Field trip to Humane Society	Compare/contrast animal treatment
Take photos	Plan for pet ownership
Interview form	Animal night
Sloppy Copy	Display projects and class book
Neat Sheet	Question and answer session

Sarah Klein is teaching a unit on animals, and the fourth–grade students have eagerly shared with the class about their pets. They have been introduced to the school's pets, two dogs from Paws With a Cause, an agency that matches service dogs with people with disabilities. The agency also sponsors pet therapy programs to train pets and owners to visit hospitals and nursing homes.

Sarah wants her students to develop an awareness and sensitivity for abandoned and relinquished animals. She wants to acquaint the class with the work of public services that are involved in the care of animals such as local animal shelters and the humane societies. She sees a perfect opportunity to use a nonfiction book that she thinks will have high interest for the students.

Shelley Swanson Sateren's book is beautifully illustrated, sensitively written, and touchingly graphic in its portrayal of the plight of many animals as well as the therapeutic and service use of animals in today's society. The book can be read in one sitting, but is well suited to reading a section a day.

Speaking and Listening

Sarah introduces the book by stimulating a discussion with the following questions:

How can we show kindness to animals?

What pets do we have?

How do we care for them?

How can pets help people?

How can we help animals?

After students share their responses, Sarah tells them that a young man from the local Humane Society is waiting outside the classroom door to speak about pets and our responsibilities to them. He enters with a Dalmatian named Max and talks about animals that either are captured because they ran away or are relinquished because the owners no longer want them or cannot care for them. He talks about the movie *One Hundred and One Dalmatians* (1961), which led many people to acquire Dalmatian puppies like Max. His family got tired of him and left him at the Humane Society. The speaker also explains the uses of animals for therapy and service.

The students' interest has been heightened, and Sarah introduces *The Humane Societies: A Voice for the Animals* by showing a few of the pictures in the book and talking about the cover.

Reading and Research

After reading the book aloud over several days after lunch, discussing each section with the class, and recording students' questions, Sarah divides the class into groups. Each group will do local research on some topics covered in the book, then produce its own chapter for a class book titled *Our Local Humane Society and Related Animal Services*. Students come up with the following chapters to develop:

Our Local Humane Society: Past and Present

Profiles on Adoptive Families

Reasons for Relinquishing Animals

Pet Therapy in Senior Citizen Centers

Paws With a Cause

Students will sign up to work on a chapter. Sources will be the Humane Society, the Internet, books in their school library, and any other community resources.

Field Trip

Sarah arranges a visit to the local Humane Society to broaden the students' knowledge and to check their research. They are permitted to take photos so they can add them to their chapters. Some students bring their own cameras, and Sarah has hers in case any group does not have a member with a camera.

Students were given an interview form (see Figure 4.9) on which to record the answers of the officials with whom they spoke. Upon returning they organize their information and prepare to write a rough draft.

Writing Process

The writing process has been in place from the beginning of this project. First, students engaged in precomposing or rehearsing through discussion. They each wrote a rough draft or "sloppy copy" of a section of the chapter on which their group was working. Group members then exchanged papers to help one another revise and edit. Because this class is becoming adept at using computers and because the school has a computer lab, Sarah arranges with the computer teacher to assist her students in putting their final copies, their "neat sheets," on the computer. With more computer time she would have them compose on the computer, and she hopes to do that another year.

Active Involvement and Service

Sarah has a principal who is very receptive to her project and is herself an animal lover. The principal obtains two dogs from Paws With a Cause. Although the principal is in charge of raising the pups, she brings them to school daily to aid in their socialization. The dogs become the school mascots, and Sarah's class becomes responsible for their care while they are at school. During this time, further research

Figure 4.9
Interview Form

What kind of animals do you receive?

_____

How many animals do you have now? _____

How many animals do you get each year? _____

How many animals are adopted?_____

What happens in the adoption interview?

_____

_____

_____

_____

Do you hear from the new owners after they adopted pets?_____

What do they say? _____

_____

_____

What can we do as a class to help you?_____

_____

_____

_____

_____

_____

(write your own question here) _____

_____

_____

leads the students to learn about the Paws With a Cause organization and to invite a representative of this organization to speak to the class. Students decide to hold their own bake sale to raise money for Paws With a Cause and their local Humane Society. Because the bake sale is successful, they decide to have one once a month and to alternate organizations to whom their proceeds will be given.

Projects

The concluding projects seem like only a beginning because there are many more connections to learning that could be made. Sarah also respects the research on multiple intelligences (Gardner, 1983; Gardner & Hatch, 1989) and wants to stimulate children to pursue a project in their own areas of interest and ability. She comes up with the following options from which they could choose:

Write a story as a Humane Society dog in the first person: Tell how you feel (see Figure 4.10).

Write a letter to the humane society asking how you can help them or expressing any concerns you have after visiting it.

Figure 4.10
Humane Society Writing Project

Dear Max,
    I hate being in here. I mean they take good care of me and all, and they have a million of other Pets to take care of, but I want special attention. I wish my owner would come back & get me! I don't desearve to go to jail! I didn't do anything wrong! Even if my owner doesn't come back I should at least be adopted. Don't you think So?

                                Love,
                                Sanuk

PS Get me out of HERE!

                                Julienne Louters, gr. 4

Diagram an ideal Humane Society facility.

Choose some suitable music (compact discs, tapes) that you would play to the animals at the Humane Society to make them feel more comfortable and calm.

Offer to walk pets in your neighborhood if you know them well and they are "people friendly." If you know neighbors such as elderly people, who are unable to take their pets for a walk, they might appreciate this opportunity for their pets to get some exercise.

Spend more time with your own pet. Engage pets in play activities outside, which is good for them and for you.

Do a research project on how animals were treated in the past. Use the comparison chart for filling in information (see Figure 4.11).

List what you do and will promise to do as a good pet owner (see Figure 4.12, see page 122).

Figure 4.11
Compare and Contrast Treatment of Animals

Questions	Past	Present
What happens/ed to stray animals?	shot or drowned	picked up
What happens/ed to unwanted pets?	chased away or killed	brought to shelter
How did people go about adopting a pet that was given up?	they didn't	go to humane society or shelter
(add your own questions)		
Why do people give up pets?		they act bad. people move

Figure 4.12
Good Pet Owner Chart

Our pets are our friends. They are our animal companions and need our love and care. Fill in the chart below for yourself or someone else you have seen care for a pet.

I Am a Good Pet Owner because…
(or _____ is a good pet owner because…)
        (name)

> Walk my dog.
> feed him.
> love him!
> talk to him.

Animal Night

Sarah's class holds an animal night for parents and community members during which students display their projects and the class book. They introduce the Paws With a Cause dogs. Each group responsible for a chapter in the book has appointed one of its members to give a brief presentation. Individual projects are displayed in the gym, and part of the evening is given to having students stand by their display to answer questions from family and community members in attendance.

Summary

Reading *The Humane Societies: A Voice for the Animals* leads to a year–long series of activities that inspires interest, contributes to students' awareness of societal issues, involves them in their local communities, and deepens their own appreciation for animals. Furthermore, it integrates listening, speaking, reading, and writing throughout the unit in meaningful communication–centered ways.

Children's Book Cited

Sateren, S.S. (1997). *The Humane Societies: A voice for the animals*. New York: Dillon Press.

Related Books

Nonfiction

Fowler, S.W. (1997). *Best friends: Portraits of rescued, sheltered, and adopted Companions*. Petaluma, CA: Voice and Vision.

Hess, E. (1998). *Lost and found: Dogs, cats and everyday heroes at a country animal shelter*. San Diego, CA: Harcourt Brace.

Fiction

Baglio, B.M. (1999). *Animal Ark #11: Owl in the office*. New York: Apple Books.

Delton, J. (1988). *Lucky dog days*. New York: Yearling.

Warner, G.C. (1991). *The animal shelter mystery: Boxcar children mystery #22*. Morton Grove, IL: Albert Whitman.

Pets

Berenstein, S., & J. (1990). *The Berenstein Bears' trouble with pets*. New York: Random House.

Caldwell, L., & Carter, N. (1999). *God made pets*. Boston: Standard Publishing.

Cecil, L. (1995). *Preposterous pets*. New York: Greenwillow.

Chrystie, F.N. (1998). *Pets: A comprehensive handbook for kids*. New York: Little, Brown.

Rogers, J. (ill.). (1997). *Weird pet poems*. New York: Simon & Schuster.

Tuxworth, N. (1998). *Let's look at pets*. New York: Anness.

Dogs

Cole, J., & Calmenson, S. (1999). *Give a dog a bone: Stories, poems, jokes, and riddles about dogs*. New York: Scholastic.

Disney, Walt. (1961). *One hundred and one dalmations* [Movie]. (Available from Walt Disney Productions)

Rosen, M., & Mosner, D. (1993). *Kid's best dog book and field guide to neighborhood dogs*. New York: Workman.

PLAY WITH POETRY WITH *THE BOOK OF PIGERICKS*

(by Arnold Lobel)

Thirty-eight pig limericks with imaginative, hog-wild illustrations invite readers and listeners to create their own limericks.

Children's Choices for 1984. Reprinted from *The Reading Teacher*, October 1984.

 Activities for This Book

Activate prior knowledge	Compose as a group
Limericks and pigericks	Read aloud to keep ideas flowing
Read and brainstorm	Illustrate kidericks
Create a kiderick	Create a class book
Writing, editing, publishing, and illustrating	Read kidericks to Grade 2
	Read *The Book of Pigericks* to Grade 2

Cullinan, Scala, and Schroeder (1995) define limericks as "a form of light verse that follows a definite pattern of five lines: the first, second, and fifth lines consist of three feet and rhyme; and the third and fourth lines consist of two feet and rhyme" (p. 38). These authors suggest that we first develop a love of poetry in students so they will be receptive and enthusiastic to poetry learning. *The Book of Pigericks* provides a humorous, fun way to introduce students to limericks. Arnold Lobel's fanciful book contains a whimsical collection, using the limerick rhyming pattern of a–a, b–b, a:

> There once was an old pig with a pen
>
> Who wrote stories and verse now and then.
>
> To enhance these creations,
>
> He drew illustrations
>
> With brushes, some paints, and his pen. (p. 9)

Each page thereafter contains a different pigerick that usually begins with "There once was a pig from…" and has an accompanying illustration.

This book remains popular today with all levels of elementary school teachers and students. It introduces students to the limerick in a lighthearted way that motivates students to compose and relieves the feelings of inadequacy that more serious and eloquent poetry can produce in children. Lobel's book is a fine addition to a curriculum that seeks to build fun and creativity in manipulating language while relieving the pressure of creating serious poetry.

Introducing Pigericks

Teachers eagerly embrace creative writing ideas that can form "quick writes," brief writing activities that take 15 minutes daily over a week or two. Quick writes enable students to engage in different kinds of writing to enjoy an aesthetic response to reading and writing (Rosenblatt, 1985) while still working on writing folders or more complex writing, such as stories or essays they are taking through the writing process.

Sam Johnson wants to ease his fourth graders into poetry. Some think poetry is either funny like Shel Silverstein's or serious like Robert Frost's. Sam thinks pigericks will ease students from the humorous to a more serious limerick, leading to more substantial poetry.

He has focus journals in which the class determines a weekly focus for a brief morning writing time. He announces "Pigericks" as this week's journal topic.

Cindy asks, "A pigerick! What's a pigerick?"

Kevin says, "It sounds like something you eat, maybe like a pig–on–a–stick."

"Oh, you mean when they roast a whole pig and put an apple in its mouth? Yuck!" Dorothy adds.

Showing his excitement over their enthusiasm and wanting to steer the conversation, Sam responds, "You are really thinking and associating. Let's talk about limericks. Who knows what a limerick is?"

Emily answers, "A kind of poem."

"Yes, what kind of a poem?" Sam questions.

Kevin says, "It probably rhymes."

Sam asks, "How does it rhyme?"

"I know! We read some for St. Patrick's Day last year. The first two lines and the last line rhyme, and the third and fourth," Julie responds.

Sam explains, "Okay class—Julie is right and the rhyme is a–a, b–b, a. I'll write that on the chalkboard. We are going to do a fun kind of limerick. It's called a 'pigerick,' and I'll read you some."

Brainstorming Pigericks

Sam reads several pigericks, inviting the class to study the illustrations of each pig. He then invites students to engage in shared and interactive writing with him, following the various ways of engaging students in teacher–assisted writing (Button, Johnson, & Fergerson, 1996). He teaches and models while receiving students' input, which is a good way to introduce a new form of writing.

After a vote, "kids" is the decided theme and "kidericks" are the poetry the class will create.

Sam writes, "There once was a kid from_____"

"What shall we say, our street, our city, our state?" he asks.

Cindy says, "Let's do Texas!"

"There once was a kid from Texas

Who_____,'" Sam continues.

"What words rhyme with *Texas*?"

Several students respond, "*Lexus, Nexus.*"

Gradually, the kiderick takes shape as the students brainstorm. Sam writes each line on the chalkboard. Students copy their class kiderick into their focus journals, and one student offers to type it on the computer and print it so the class kiderick will become the center item on the bulletin board. The class kiderick is placed inside the outline of a pig (see Figure 4.13).

Sam attaches a curly tail, which is actually a plastic pull strip from an orange-juice can. The students love it and ask if they can have one to attach to their pigs when they write their kidericks. The class decides to paste their kidericks on the shapes of pigs, in honor of *The Book*

Figure 4.13
Kiderick in a Pig

There once was a kid from Texas,
Whose dad drove around in a Lexus
The wind blew his hair
And made his head bare
And he lost his account with Nexus!

of Pigericks, which inspired them and stands next to the bulletin board. "This way we'll give credit to Arnold Lobel whose idea we took in making our kidericks!" announces Courtney.

Peer Publishing

Sam forms groups of students to compose a kiderick together. One group member serves as the scribe, while the others suggest ideas. Each group revises, edits, and word–processes their kiderick to share with the class (see Figure 4.14, page 128). They also write their group's final product in their focus journals. One or two group members become the illustrators for the copy that will be published in the class book. Each group will also produce a kiderick in the shape of a pig and attach it to the class bulletin board around the class kiderick.

Figure 4.14
More Kidericks From Grade 4

There was a young fella from Pella
Who met a young teacher quite "bella"
"I wonder," said he,
"If she would marry me.
Then I would be one happy fella."

There once was a kid from Sarnia
Who always read books from Narnia
Though the characters were great
He did all of them hate
'Cause from reading, he got a "harnia."

By the second week students are eager to hear a pigerick each day, which was how Sam had begun each day the previous week. "A pigerick is like a vitamin," he said. "It gives you energy to write."

Students write their own kidericks about themselves using a street, a county, a continent, a river, or whatever they could identify. They write in their focus journals and confer with peers and Sam. A class "yelp-and-help" time allows anyone to call for help with a line if they are stuck. By the end of this week, students are ready to copy from their focus journals and publish their independently written kidericks and self-portrait illustrations. Sam laminates each and puts them in a class book, *The Kids in Grade 4 Create Kidericks*.

Sharing With Grade 2

A final activity involves the class reading their kidericks with their second-grade buddies. Frequently, grades 2 and 4 get together to share reading and writing.

"Can we read them some pigericks, too?" asks Brea.

"Sure," responds Sam, and several class members volunteer to read a pigerick to the whole Grade 2 class. There are some giggles from the second graders.

"I don't think they get the pigericks," said Bill. "They giggled because of the dressed up, funny pigs, but they didn't get what a pigerick is."

"But you do—and now we can go on to limericks," replies Sam. "You're ready for bigger and better things. Shall we take one more week to read different kinds of limericks and write some more?"

The class unanimously agrees.

Summary

Sam and his fourth graders used a simple, light–hearted book as an introduction to a form of poetry. They engaged in whole–class, small–group, buddy, and individual work with reading, writing, listening, and sharing. Teacher modeling with shared and interactive writing resulted in learning together. Most important, perhaps, was the enthusiasm generated for more reading and writing of limericks, which would carry over to other forms of poetry.

Children's Books Cited

Lobel, A. (1983). *The book of pigericks*. New York: Harper & Row.

Children's Limerick Books

Lear, E. (1992). *Daffy down dilles: Silly limericks*. Honesdale, PA: Boyds Mills Press.
Livingston, M.C. (1991). *Lots of limericks*. New York: Margaret McElderry.
Roehl, M. (1996). *A carousel of limericks*. Blue Ridge Summit, PA: Vestal Press.

More Limerick Books

Ash, J.D. (1997). *Potpourri of the mind: A collection of poems in the limerick style*. Weston, CT: Old Pine Books.
Ash, J.D. (1997). *Sojourn in limerick: Poetic limericks visited once again*. Weston, CT: Old Pine Books.
Deex, A., Nesbit, W., & Smith, V.W. (Eds.). (1995). *Off the limerick bush: 288 original limericks by contemporary authors*. Lakeside, CA: Big Blue Books.
Manley, M. (1994). *Talkaty talker: Limericks*. Honesdale, PA: Boyds Mills Press.
Perrine, L., Berardo, P., & Smith, V.W. (Eds.). (1993). *Into the limerick grove*. Palo Alto, CA: Zapizdat Publications.
Reed, L. (1996). *Complete limerick book*. Detroit, MI: Omnigraphics.
Smith, V.W. (1991). *Under the limerick tree: 144 original limericks*. Palo Alto, CA: Zapizdat Publications.

Three Cinderella Stories

VASILISSA THE BEAUTIFUL: A RUSSIAN FOLKTALE

(adapted by Elizabeth Winthrop, ill. by Alexander Koshkin)

A beautifully illustrated retelling of a Russian fairy tale about the beautiful Vasilissa and her struggles with her wicked stepmother and stepsisters. Vasilissa uses her magic doll to escape from the witch Baba Yaga. Children love this story reminiscent of "Cinderella" and "Hansel and Gretel."

Children's Choices for 1992. Reprinted from *The Reading Teacher*, October 1992.

YEH–SHEN: A CINDERELLA STORY FROM CHINA

(by Ai-Ling Louie, ill. by Ed Young)

As the title indicates, this is a Chinese version of the familiar Cinderella story. Older readers were intrigued by Ed Young's imaginative watercolor and pastel illustrations and by this version of the story. Younger readers simply enjoy the story for its own sake.

Children's Choices for 1983. Reprinted from *The Reading Teacher*, October 1983.

CINDERELLA (FAY'S FAIRY TALES)

(retold by William Wegman, with Carole Kismaric and Marvin Heiferman, ill. by William Wegman)

A true classic presented in a refreshing way, using dogs as the main characters and other animals in supporting roles. The dazzling photographs and visual interpretation renew the spirit of Cinderella, making it a story for all ages. A first grader remarked, "It was so funny!"

Children's Choices for 1994. Reprinted from *The Reading Teacher*, October 1994.

 Activities for These Books

Story elements	Compose questions and answers
Settings	Post books on bulletin board
Location on globe	Share questions and answers
Stravinsky's "Firebird"	Compare/Contrast chart
Mussorgsky's "Pictures at an Exhibition"	Predict about Cinderella
Ideas from cover	Brainstorming other Cinderella possibilities
Teacher read aloud	Student versions
Cinderella Flap Books	

Cinderella has been delighting children for hundreds of years, far longer than the most familiar version has existed. Recently, many teachers have taken a renewed interest in Cinderella tales because of the variety of ways they can be used in the classroom to study different cultures. They permit opportunity for comparing and contrasting by examining similarities and differences among the tales. As Worthy and Bloodgood (1992/1993) found, "connecting the known stories to new, structurally similar ones is a powerful tool for reading instruction and an excellent foundation for exploring other subjects through literature" (p. 290).

The Cinderella tales suggest a universal theme that good triumphs over evil, most often in a family setting. Because of the multiple levels of interpretation, they are suitable for all ages. There are at least 1,500 different versions throughout the world. The first versions are considered to be the story of Yeh–Shen, which originated in China over 1,000 years ago, and the story of Rhodopis, a Greek slave who became the wife of an Egyptian pharaoh, and whose sandal is the first recorded version of the slipper test for choosing a bride (Pike, Compain, & Mumper, 1997).

The diversity of heroines, evil characters, magical forces, and means of restoring the heroine provide a fascinating study of the cultures from which the tales originate. The familiar American version most closely resembles the French version by Charles Perrault with a meek and mild heroine, wicked stepmother and stepsisters, fairy godmother, and a handsome prince. Walt Disney (1968, 1971, 1974) popularized the beautiful blonde heroine and the handsome prince. By contrast, the heroines Princess Furball in *Princess Furball* and Blanche in *The Talking Eggs* are strong and in control. Magical helpers vary, including a kind, elderly woman in *The Talking Eggs*, a conjure woman in *Moss Gown*, monks in *Little Sister and the Month Brothers*, a little doll in the Russian tale *Vasilissa the Beautiful*, and a variety of animals including fish in some Asian accounts, such as *Yeh–Shen* and *The Korean Cinderella*.

Villains vary from a wicked father in *Princess Furball*, a rejecting father in *Moss Gown*, to a group of servants in *The Egyptian Cinderella*. The well-known rescuing prince is a warrior in the Native American versions of *Sootface* and *The Turkey Girl*, a hard working farmer in *Little Sister and the Month Brothers*, a tsar in *Vasilissa the Beautiful*, and a pharaoh in *The Egyptian Cinderella*.

Even the universal theme of love originates in different ways after a test or challenge for the young girl. In the Native American versions, *Sootface* and *The Rough Face Girl*, the young girl who can see the invisible being, the warrior, becomes his squaw. In *The Egyptian Cinderella*, a falcon delivers a slipper to the pharaoh who then seeks its owner and marries her. For Vasilissa the test is to weave flax into linen and sew shirts for the Tsar. She also must endure the witch, Baba Yaga.

In recent years "fractured fairy tales," spoofs or parodies of Cinderella and other fairy tales, have delighted children with their humor and clever distortions of the familiar tale such as *Cinder-Elly*, a poetic New York City version. *Cinderella* (*Fay's Fairy Tales*) tells a fairly traditional Cinderella story with dogs as the characters.

JoAnn Van Vugt is a third–grade teacher in a small private school. Every year she engages her primary students in several versions of Cinderella. Jo's school population contains children from a middle class suburban area. Many of the children in her classroom come from families in which both parents work, and one child comes from a single-parent family. Reading is important to many of these parents, and Jo has good support in having the children read at home in the evening. The children are active readers, working toward their reading goal in the Book It! (Pizza Hut) program, and also doing book reports for the classroom. She knows that all the children are familiar with the Cinderella story, so she wants to make them aware of the many versions of this story. Another objective of reading these versions is to make the children more aware of other cultures in the world, which provides an opportunity to develop one aspect of critical thinking (Beyer, 1988): comparing and contrasting.

Story Elements and Settings

Before beginning the actual lesson, Jo has the children brainstorm and chart the elements found in the traditional Cinderella story. She leaves space for adding the elements from other versions of this story, which will be filled in as the versions are read (see Figure 4.15, page 134).

A special bag has been placed in the library that contains many versions of the Cinderella story that the children may read and enjoy. Among these books are versions from Korea, Ireland, and Italy, some Native American versions, and a modern poetic version set in New York City. The students have been told that there are many versions of Cinderella that are all a bit different, which possibly has piqued their enthusiasm for investigating the books.

Jo has the students sit on the floor around a world globe. She leads them in discussion about where the continent of Asia is and where the country of Russia is. She plays a compact disc of Stravinsky's "The Firebird," a Russian fairytale, to create the mood and provide some cultur-

Figure 4.15
Chart for Comparing and Contrasting Cinderella Stories

Title-Author/ Origin-Setting	Main Characters	Cause of lowly position	Quest or desire	How wish is granted	Where/ how the hero is met	Challenge	Conclusion

Adapted from Pike, K., Compain, R., & Mumper, J. (1997). *New connections: An integrated approach to literacy* (2nd ed.). New York: Addison-Wesley Longman.

al connections to Russia. The students find their own country to see how far the United States is from Russia.

They discuss that in Russia a tsar was like a king or prime minister in other countries. Jo plays a compact disc of Mussorgsky's "Pictures at an Exhibition," the segment about Baba Yaga's hut on chicken legs. It is important to give students several ways in which they can visualize the story, and hearing the music helps them to think about the setting in Russia. While listening, the children shut their eyes and try to imagine what it must look like. After listening to the music, they discuss who Baba Yaga is and how this character plays a role in Russian culture. On a small table Jo has placed paper plates with dried peas, poppy seeds, and flax for the children to examine. Each is labeled because these are words that play a part in this story. Also on the table are a small mortar and pestle for the children to examine.

Reading Aloud

Jo reads the beginning of *Vasilissa the Beautiful* aloud to the children as they follow along in their own copies. She introduces the book and has the children look at the cover. She asks them to predict what will happen in this story.

"I think Vasilissa will have evil stepsisters," says Esther.

"I think she will be very poor," says Paul, "and have an evil stepparent."

"I see a prince on a beautiful horse," says Sue, "so I think she will meet a prince."

"Let's read and find out," says Jo. "As we read, remember to see how this story compares to the traditional Cinderella story."

She begins reading the story aloud while the children follow along. Esther is surprised to hear about the doll that Vasilissa's mother gives her. She comments that this is different from the familiar Cinderella.

Jo continues to read aloud to the children, occasionally stopping to check comprehension or to ask for a prediction. Sometimes she asks for volunteers to help her read aloud.

Comparing and Contrasting Cinderella Stories

Jo starts by showing students a chart that is designed to compare several Cinderella stories. Together they review what they did yesterday by filling in the chart for *Vasilissa the Beautiful* (see Figure 4.16, page 136).

"Today, class, we are going to read another version of Cinderella written in the country of China many years ago," says Jo. "It seems that this version was written before the other European versions." They examine the globe to locate China.

"Even though the countries, Russia and China, are next to each other, you'll find the stories are very different!" Jo predicts.

"How is Yeh–Shen different from Vasilissa the Beautiful?" asks Esther. "Is it just the names?"

Thomas asks, "Does she look like the Cinderella we know or does she look like a person from China?"

Before reading, Jo explains that people in many Asian countries believe that spirits live in the bodies of animals and can help people when

Figure 4.16
Completed Chart for Comparing and
Contrasting Cinderella Stories

Title-Author/ Origin-Setting	Main Characters	Cause of lowly position	Quest or desire	How wish is granted	Where/ how the hero is met	Challenge	Conclusion
Vasilissa the beautiful. Elizabeth Winthrop Russian	Vasilissa Father Stepmother 2 stepsisters Baba Yaga old woman +sar	mistreated by her Stepmother and 2 stepsisters	to survive	a magical doll	Vasilissa meets the tsar at the palace	She must weave shirts from flax	Vasilissa marries the tsar
Yeh-shen Ai-Ling Louie China	Yeh Shen Stepmother Stepsister	Yeh-shen's father dies	to go to the festival	magical fish bones	they meet at the pavilion during the search for the owner of the lost slipper	whether or not the slipper fits	Yeh-shen marries the King
Cinderella William Wegman magical dog Kingdom	Ella (Cinderella) Father Stepmother 2 stepsisters fairy godmother prince	Ella's father dies, Stepmother and step-sisters mistreat her	to go to the ball	fairy godmother	at the Palace ball	Whether or not the glass slipper fit	Ella marries the prince

Adapted from Pike, K., Compain, R., & Mumper, J. (1997). *New connections: An integrated approach to literacy* (2nd ed.). New York: Addison-Wesley Longman.

they are in trouble. She asks the children to listen for the animals that contain spirits. Then she begins reading *Yeh–Shen: A Cinderella Story From China.*

When they finish, the children help Jo fill in the chart for this version of the story. They also talk about the animal that helped Yeh–Shen and what character from the familiar version it resembles. Some of the children, remembering the traditional version of Cinderella, suggest that the fish is similar to the fairy godmother.

To further enhance the third–grade skill of comparing and contrasting, Jo asks the children to write a paragraph comparing the doll in *Vasilissa the Beautiful* to the fish in *Yeh–Shen.* She encourages the children to start with a main idea sentence. The class brainstorms some possible sentences while Jo writes the possibilities on the board. She reminds students to indent the first line and to remember that all the other sentences should relate back to the main idea. They are encouraged to have at least four other sentences in their paragraphs.

Jo asks the children to think of other possible versions of Cinderella and to come up with characters to represent the fairy godmother, the wicked stepmother and stepsisters, the prince, and Cinderella. They list these ideas on the board. The children suggest other countries that might have a version of the story. They also think of modern versions of the story. Then Jo asks them what they would include in a Cinderella story if they were to write one. She tells the class that there are over a thousand different versions of the story and that they have come up with some ideas that actually exist in a version. She shows them some that she has collected and puts them on the table for them to read during quiet reading time (see More Cinderella Books, p. 101).

Jo holds up the book *Cinderella (Fay's Fairy Tales)* by William Wegman. She asks students to predict from the picture what this version will be like and how similar or different it is from the versions they have already read.

"Well," says Jackie, "for one thing it looks like Cinderella is a dog."

"Why do you say that?" says Jo.

"I think that because there is a dog sitting in a carriage looking like a princess," says Jackie, "and it looks kind of silly."

Jo solicits other predictions from the children as to what this version will be like and why they think so, listing some on the board for future reference. Then Jo reads the story, and they underline the predictions that came true.

Together they discuss this latest version of Cinderella and fill in the class comparison chart (see Figure 4.2). They look at the pictures in the three books and discuss how different each of them is. As they do this, the children also share some of the Cinderella books they have been reading from the reading table. Jo suggests that they pair up with classmates who read the same version and together fill in a row of the comparison chart for other Cinderella stories.

Creating Cinderella Flap Books

"Now we are going to make Cinderella Flap Books with our partners," says Jo (see Figures 4.17a & b). "Cut out both parts of Cinderella and then cut the dotted flaps on her skirt. Then glue the back and front together leaving the flaps free. Talk together and think of eight questions about *Vasilissa the Beautiful* and write them on the flaps. Be careful to think of questions that you know the answers to because you also will have to write the answers underneath the flap. When that is done, you can color the book together. We will staple the booklets to the bulletin board so that you can share them with the rest of the class." The children chatter quietly about their books as they come up with questions and answers. This activity puts the story more vividly in their minds as they focus on questions and supply answers.

Figure 4.17a
Cinderella Flap Book

Reprinted with permission of Teacher Created Materials.

Figure 4.17b
Cinderella Flap Book

1. Duplicate the Cinderella patterns onto large construction paper or index stock.

2. Cut the flaps on the dotted lines.

3. Glue the front and back Cinderella together, taking care not to glue down the flaps.

4. Direct the students to write on each flap, and have them lift up the flap to illustrate the text.

Suggested Uses

- Pair or group the students. Tell them to write a question about the Cinderella fairy tale on each flap. Lift up the flap to write the answer. Have the students trade their Cinderella books with another group.

- Read *Mufaro's Beautiful Daughters* by John Steptoe to the class. Compare the story with Cinderella. Have the students write one fact from Cinderella on each flap. Tell them to lift up the flaps and write a parallel fact from *Mufaro's Beautiful Daughters.*

Example

Cinderella has 2 stepsisters.	Manyora and Nyasha are two beautiful sisters.

- Direct the students to write a Cinderella story with a different setting. You may want to read other versions of the fairy tale to give them some ideas of how to change the story. A good resource to use is *Yeh Shen: A Cinderella Story from China* retold by Al-Ling Louie.

Bear Essentials: A Newspaper of Creative Ideas for K-5 Teachers   Volume 1 • Number 1 • January/February 1993

As the booklets are stapled to the bulletin board, the children are encouraged to visit the bulletin board Cinderellas, read the questions, and try to answer them before checking the answers that are provided under the flaps. Sometimes one partner will read the question and the other partner will read the answer.

Creating Versions of Cinderella

"Let's think about some possibilities for Cinderella stories that we might write," says Jo. The children give examples of some of the ideas. Jackie really likes the idea of an animal as the Cinderella figure, so she suggests the idea of a pig. Thomas thinks it would be interesting to have a Cinderella story in outer space with an astronaut as the prince. Esther likes putting Cinderella in a different setting also, but she thinks about a Pilgrim Cinderella because they just finished studying the Pilgrims for Thanksgiving.

The children begin to write their versions of Cinderella. They use the chart on the wall comparing all the stories they have read to help them think of story elements to include. As they write, they help each other edit what they have written. Jo reminds them to read over what they have written with a "one-foot" voice (Collins, 1992), which is loud enough to be heard only by someone one foot away and not the rest of the class. After they have the first draft written and edited by several peers, the children write a second draft. A mother volunteer helps the class publish their stories using the computer so the children are reminded that they have to write the way they want them typed. Then, they create a picture to illustrate their Cinderella stories. All the stories are laminated and included in a book to be displayed in the classroom library.

Summary

Jo has inspired interest in Cinderella tales, which will continue throughout the school year. She has engaged her class in a variety of reading and writing activities along with critical thinking. She has enlarged their worlds by showing a similar tale from other cultures and she has encouraged creative thinking by including a "spoof" Cinderella. She has paved the way for further cultural studies as well as additional fairy tale studies.

More Cinderella Tales

Climo, S. (1989). *The Egyptian Cinderella*. New York: HarperCollins.
Climo, S. (1993). *The Korean Cinderella*. New York: HarperCollins.
Climo, S. (1996). *The Irish Cinderlad*. New York: HarperCollins.

Climo, S. (1999). *The Persian Cinderella*. New York: HarperCollins.

Compton, J. (1994). *An Appalachian American tale*. New York: Holiday House.

Delamare, D. (1993). *Cinderella*. New York: Simon & Schuster. (Italian Cinderella tale)

Dematons, C. (1996). *Looking for Cinderella*. Asheville, NC: Front Street. (Dutch Cinderella tale)

Disney, W. (1968). *Cinderella*. New York: Golden Books.

Disney, W. (1971). *"Cinderella." The new Walt Disney treasury: 10 favorite stories*. New York: Golden Books.

Disney W. (1974). *Cinderella, Disney's wonderful world of reading*. New York: Random House.

Grimm, The Brothers. (1994). *Cinderella*. Owings Mills, MD: Ottenheimer Publishing. (Traditional Cinderella tale)

Hague, M. (1989). *Cinderella and other tales from Perrault*. New York: Henry Holt. (French Cinderella tale)

Han, O.S. (1996). *Kongi and Potgi*. New York: Dial Books. (Korean Cinderella tale)

Hooks, W.H. (1986). *Moss gown*. St. Louis, MO: Clarion Books. (A tale of the American Plantation South)

Huck, C. (1989). *Princess Furball*. New York: Scholastic. (A European tale)

Johnston, T. (1998). *Bigfoot CindeRRRRRella*. New York: Scholastic.

Karlin, B. (1989). *Cinderella*. New York: Trumpet. (Retelling of the Cinderella tale)

Louie, A. (1982). *Yeh–Shen*. New York: Philomel Books. (Chinese Cinderella tale)

Lum, D. (1994). *The golden slipper*. Mahwah, NJ: Troll Associates. (Vietnamese Cinderella legend)

Marlin, R., & Shannon, D. (1992). *The rough–faced girl*. New York: Putnam. (An Algonquin Cinderella tale)

Minters, F. (1994). *Cinder–Elly*. New York: Penguin.

Munsch, R.N. (1980). *The paper bag princess*. Buffalo, NY: Annick Press.

Paterson, K. (1992). *The king's equal*. New York: Trumpet. (European Cinderella tale)

Perlman, J. (1992). *Cinderella penguin, or, the little glass flipper*. New York: Scholastic. (Fractured Fairy tale)

Pollack, P. (1996). *The turkey girl*. Boston: Little, Brown. (Zuni Cinderella story)

San Souci, R.D. (1989). *The talking eggs*. New York: Scholastic. (African American folk tale)

San Souci, R.D. (1994). *Sootface*. New York: Doubleday. (Ojibwa Indian Cinderella story)

San Souci, R.D. (1998). *Cendrillon*. New York: Simon & Schuster. (Caribbean Cinderella story)

Schenk de Regniers, B. (1976). *Little Sister and the Month Brothers*. New York: Mulberry Books. (Slavic tale)

Schroeder, A. (1997). *Smoky Mountain Rose*. New York: Dial Books. (Appalachian American tale)

Silverman, E. (1999). *Raisel's riddle*. New York: Farrar, Straus & Giroux. (Jewish re–telling of the Cinderella story)

Steptoe, J. (1987). *Mufaro's beautiful daughters*. New York: Scholastic. (African tale)

Wegman, W. (1993). *Cinderella (Fay's Fairy Tales)*. New York: Hyperion Books. (Cinderella tale featuring dogs)

Winthrop, E. (1991). *Vasilissa the Beautiful*. New York: HarperCollins. (Russian folk tale)

Yorinks, A. (1989). *Ugh*. New York: Trumpet. (Stone–Aged Cinderella story)

Music References

Mussorsgsky/Ravel. *Pictures at an exhibition*. [Recorded by Chicago Symphony Orchestra]. [CD]. London: Jubilee. (1988)

Stravinsky, I. *The Firebird*. [Recorded by Seattle Symphony, narrated by Natalia Makarova]. [CD]. Hollywood, CA: Delos. (1991)

Books Used With
OLDER READERS

PHILIP HALL LIKES ME. I RECKON MAYBE.

SEEDFOLKS

TOPS AND BOTTOMS

DRAGONWINGS

CAN'T YOU MAKE THEM BEHAVE, KING GEORGE?

WILL YOU SIGN HERE, JOHN HANCOCK?

WHAT'S THE BIG IDEA, BEN FRANKLIN?

GEORGE WASHINGTON'S MOTHER

Books Used With Older Readers

THINK THROUGH RELATIONSHIPS WITH *PHILIP HALL LIKES ME. I RECKON MAYBE.*

(by Bette Greene, ill. by Charles Lilly)

This is a warm story of a black family in Arkansas and a school girl's university escapades with clubs, parties, and competition. Upper grade black girls became attached to the book and claimed it as their own.

Classroom Choices for 1974. Reprinted from *The Reading Teacher*, November 1975.

📖 Activities for This Book

Theme: Friendship	Graph produce
Teacher read aloud	Compute expenses
Construct character webs	Guide reading and thinking
Compare lifestyles	Discuss picket lines
Illustrate the chapter	Read critically
Predict, read, and verify	Respond and reflect
Read together	Respond to behavior
Solve the character's problem	Write and share reflections
Extend character webs	Three-Level Guide
Identify with the characters	Create an ending
K–W–L	Chart predictions
Research allergies	Complete character webs and
Graphing and problem solving	illustrate final chapter

Bridget Freese is a future teacher doing preservice teaching in an urban fifth–grade classroom. She found *Philip Hall Likes Me. I Reckon Maybe* to be an engaging book about a young girl, Beth, who is trying to understand her relationship with Philip, a classmate. Beth and Philip become involved in different adventures that test their relationship much the same as most children their age. Bridget sees an opportunity for students to identify with Beth and Philip and thus increase their motivation to read. She also involves her students in thinking analytically and critically about the content. Because Bridget's fifth–grade class is composed of African American children and Caucasian children, an important feature of the book is that one of the main characters is African American and the other is Caucasian.

Bridget conducts her teaching and learning activities chapter by chapter, similar to literature studies in the older grades. She chooses activities that will evoke both an efferent and aesthetic stance (Rosenblatt, 1985). She includes strategies to aid comprehension like semantic webbing (Vacca, Vacca, & Gove, 2000), K–W–L (Ogle, 1986), comparing and contrasting with the big H (Farris, 1997), and elements of the Directed Reading-Thinking Activity (Stauffer, 1975).

Introducing the Theme

Bridget begins by having the students discuss how they can tell that someone likes them or wants to be their friend. She asks how they might respond to these indications. She reads the first chapter aloud to the children, telling the class to listen for evidence of Philip's feelings toward Beth. After reading, she asks them to describe what they thought were Philip's true feelings for Beth and to provide examples to support their ideas.

The students then discuss the characters they encountered up to this point in the story, and they formulate character webs for them. These webs will be embellished with each subsequent chapter until, at the conclusion of the story, a complete picture of the characters will emerge (see Figure 5.1).

Students are then invited to create a big H (Farris, 1997), comparing and contrasting aspects of their lives with the characters in the story (see Figure 5.2, page 148). The big H resembles the familiar Venn diagram but adds variety to a familiar task. Bridget asks students to choose Beth or Philip. "Let's say that the H stands for Hall, the name of a main character," suggests Bridget. "On each side, list characteristics of Philip or Beth, whomever you chose, that differ from you. In the middle, list characteristics that you have in common with him or her. For example, in Beth's case, she lives in the south, has to walk miles to catch her bus, and eats grits for breakfast. Compare and contrast your life with hers." In addition, at the end of each chapter the students make their own illustrations to visually represent the events of each chapter.

Predicting, Reading, and Verifying

Working in groups of four, the students engage in paired reading of Chapter 2 up to the part where Beth is trying to figure out what has happened to her father's missing turkeys. The students are familiar with the DRTA and engage in some informal predicting, reading, and proving. Then they formulate creative solutions as to how they might solve the problem. After sharing proposed solutions, the children are motivated to read the remainder of the chapter to verify or refute their

Figure 5.1
Character Web

Philip Hall Likes Me. I Reckon Maybe.
by Bette Greene

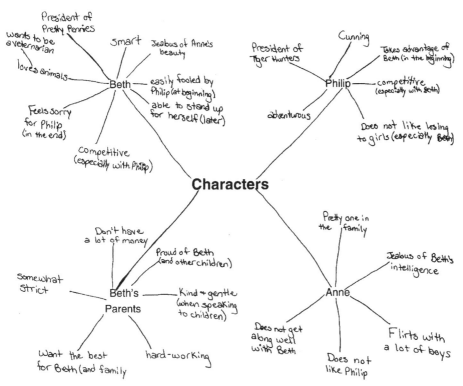

predicted solutions and see if they solved the problem as the characters did in the book.

Once again students add information to their character webs and illustrate this chapter.

Identifying With the Characters

A lively discussion about allergies serves as the class begins Chapter 3. Everyone in the class seems to have an allergy, and the children try to find an allergy worse than others mentioned. Information is listed in a

Figure 5.2
Comparing and Contrasting a Character

Philip Hall Likes Me. I Reckon Maybe.
by Bette Greene

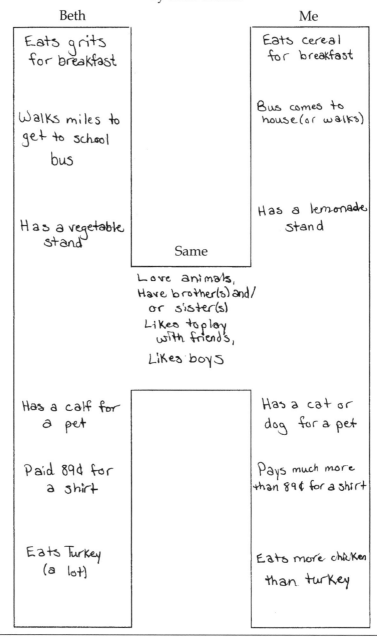

Beth

Eats grits
for breakfast

Walks miles to
get to school
bus

Has a vegetable
stand

Me

Eats cereal
for breakfast

Bus comes to
house (or walks)

Has a lemonade
stand

Same

Love animals,
Have brother(s) and/
or sister(s)
Likes to play
with friends,
Likes boys

Has a calf for
a pet

Paid 89¢ for
a shirt

Eats Turkey
(a lot)

Has a cat or
dog for a pet

Pays much more
than 89¢ for a shirt

Eats more chicken
than turkey

K–W–L chart, and students identify what they know and what they want to know. As they read the chapter and list what they have learned, they find some questions unanswered. The students decide that finding additional information about allergies would be a great research project. Several set out to find out more on the topic, and they share their findings the following week in oral presentations.

The character webs and illustrations are once again brought up to date, a task students look forward to. Initially, Bridget thought they would tire of doing a repetitious task, but instead, they enjoy illustrating and seeing how the qualities of the characters develop throughout the story.

Graphing and Problem Solving

Bridget has the students construct graphs to indicate how much produce is sold each month in Chapter 4 of *Philip Hall Likes Me. I Reckon Maybe*. The students design line graphs, pie graphs, and bar graphs to indicate how many watermelons, tomatoes, and how much corn Beth sold during a 3-month period in the book.

Students also figure out the quantity of vegetables Beth would need to sell to pay for her first year of college, using the prices of the vegetables and the cost of one year of college. Students solve this problem in many different ways, which they write in their journals and share with the class. The students gain insight into how expensive college can be and how difficult it is to be financially prepared. This activity concludes with each group suggesting how to raise money to pay for the first year of college. Work on the character webs and illustrations concludes Chapter 4.

Guided Reading and Thinking

A discussion of picket lines, what they are, and why they are used introduces students to Chapter 5. As the class reads the chapter together, Bridget guides the children through the material, asking them questions that require a more critical look at the reading material, reading beyond the lines to understand the message of the author. After completing the chapter, the students talk about how pickets were used in this story. They also discuss the effectiveness of picket lines in general and the effect of Beth's picket line in particular. They look at the picket line from the cause-effect perspective and identify some reasons for their use and effectiveness. Webs and illustrations once again bring closure to the reading of Chapter 5.

Responding and Reflecting

The students love talking about picnics, although the church picnics in the story are unfamiliar to them. However, they all relate personal accounts of picnics and exchange details of their experiences. At a church picnic described in Chapter 6, Beth helps Philip and he responds in an unusual manner. Students discuss how Philip acted when Beth helped him and why he responded as he did. A heated debate ensues as the students search for the motivation for Philip's behavior. The discussion provides valuable insights into the interpersonal relationships of the class as they relate their personal feelings to Philip's behavior. Though not intended, this discussion allows Bridget and her class to recognize the extent of their identification with Beth and Philip.

Students then reflect on their own experiences. Bridget asks, "Have you ever known something but no one would listen or believe you?" Their reflections become a journal entry that they share during Writers' Workshop.

Bridget hands out a three–level guide with statements students check to reflect their literal, interpretive, and applied comprehension (see Figure 5.3). These statements provide the basis for more reflection and discussion. They also serve as a measure of students' comprehension.

Writing a Possible Ending

Each child reads a portion of Chapter 7. At a designated stopping place, the students do an unfinished writing: "If I were Beth/Philip, I would feel...." The students support their feelings by citing evidence from the story and from their own lives.

Figure 5.3
Three-Level Guide

151

CHAPTER 5

Philip Hall Likes Me. I Reckon Maybe.
by Bette Greene

Literal Level — Check the items that explicitly represent some of the important details and actions in the story.

_____ 1. Beth's mother and father like Philip Hall.

_____ 2. Philip Hall played his guitar while Beth cleaned and worked in his father's barn.

_____ 3. Philip saved Beth from missing the bus.

_____ 4. Beth expected to get invited to Philip's party and even promised her friends invitations.

_____ 5. Beth is second in her class only to Philip Hall.

_____ 6. Philip is president of the Tiger Hunters.

_____ 7. After the day that Beth called Philip a "fraidy cat," he never spoke to her again.

Interpretive Level — Several statements below may represent what the author means. If you think any of the statements are reasonable inferences and conclusions, put a check on the line provided. Be ready to support your answers with proof from the book.

_____ 1. Philip seems to be taking advantage of Beth's friendship.

_____ 2. Philip is number one in school only because Beth lets him and doesn't try her hardest.

_____ 3. Philip would have invited Beth to the party even if she hadn't said anything to him about being a "fraidy cat."

_____ 4. Beth looked so sick to her mother because she was so sad and unhappy about what had happened between her and Philip.

_____ 5. Philip wants Beth to approve of him, respect him, and be his friend again.

_____ 6. Philip isn't going to take advantage of Beth's friendship again.

Applied Level — To apply what you read means to take information and ideas from what you have read and connect it to what you already know. If you think the statements below are supported by statements in Section II or by your previous knowledge, place a check in the blank provided. Be sure you have good reasons to justify your answers if called upon to do so.

_____ 1. It is important to stand up for what is important to you.

_____ 2. One should not take advantage of someone's friendship.

_____ 3. Your friends always know what is best for you.

_____ 4. A joke is a joke and is funny no matter who it may hurt.

_____ 5. Don't be afraid to show your feelings for someone.

Created by Amy Admiraal Libolt. Reprinted with permission.

Bridget asks the students to predict what will happen with Beth and Philip and to give reasons for their predictions, which are written on a chart. After finishing the story, they compare the end with their predicted endings. Questions guide the discussion:

> Would you have ended the book the same way the author did?
>
> How would you have written the ending?

Predictions are verified or refuted and general responses to the book are entertained.

To conclude the study *of Philip Hall Likes Me. I Reckon Maybe*, the students revisit the character webs they worked on throughout the story. In addition to summarizing the character traits of each person in the book, they discuss which character they related to and why. As a final experience the students compile their illustrations to form their own picture books. Although Bridget's preservice teaching ends here, she sees possibilities for creating more adventures for Philip and Beth with her fifth graders or for new interactions with books that have equally appealing characters.

Summary

Bridget and her fifth graders enjoyed literacy experiences that triggered critical thinking and responding. They empathized with the characters and related Beth's and Philip's experiences to their own. They responded and reflected orally and in writing. By conducting a chapter study, they simulated the kind of literature study that occurs in upper grades. They are well on their way to providing more adventures for Philip Hall and his friends, or to beginning an in–depth study of another book with equally appealing characters.

Books by Bette Greene

The drowning of Stephan Jones. (1997). Des Plaines, IL: Starfire.
Get on out of here, Philip Hall. (1999). New York: Puffin.
Philip Hall likes me. I reckon maybe. (1974). New York: Dial Books.
Summer of my German soldier. (1999). New York: Puffin.

Related Children's Books

Armstrong, W. (1969). *Sounder*. New York: Scholastic.

Armstrong, W. (1992). *Sour land*. New York: HarperCollins.

Curtis, C.P. (1995). *The Watsons go to Birmingham: 1963*. New York: Delacorte Press.

Curtis, C.P. (1999). *Bud, not Buddy*. New York: Delacorte Press.

Guy, R. (1993). *The ups and downs of Carl Davis III*. New York: Yearling Books.

Guy, R. (1996). *The friends*. New York: Bantam Books.

Hansen, J. (1991). *Yellow Bird and me*. St. Louis, MO: Clarion Books.

Moore, E. (1990). *Whose side are you on?* Gordonsville, VA: Sunburst.

Related Children's Books by Mildred Taylor

The friendship. (1987). New York: Dial Books

The gold Cadillac. (1987). New York: Dial Books

Let the circle be unbroken. (1981). New York: Dial Books

The road to Memphis. (1990). New York: Puffin.

Roll of thunder, hear my cry. (1976). New York: Dial Books.

Song of the trees. (1975). New York: Dial Books

The well. (1995). New York: Dial Books

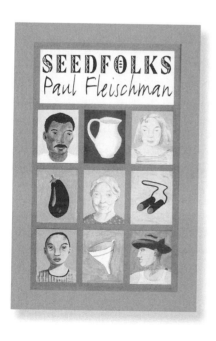

GROW WITH
SEEDFOLKS

(by Paul Fleischman, ill. by Judy Pedersen)

Thirteen characters from a multiethnic working class neighborhood in Cleveland, Ohio, tell personal stories about an ugly vacant lot that becomes a beautiful community garden. The work of planting, watering, and cultivating heals the people as well as the land.

Children's Choices for 1998. Reprinted from *The Reading Teacher*, October 1998.

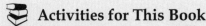 **Activities for This Book**

Get acquainted

Our uniqueness

Characters in *Seedfolks*

Critical thinking

Compare and contrast

Fill in a Double Diamond

Estimating seeds

Supporting and checking estimates

Planting information: Conditions and climate

Hearing from experts: Farmers and greenhouse operators

Geography: Global awareness

Where the characters come from

Where plants and vegetables grow

Science, writing, and illustrating

Seed parts

Our outer shells and inner selves

Shari Faber, Dena Velderman, and Louise Verhoef are future teachers who are doing a reading practicum with fourth- through sixth–grade students in a large urban public school district. They have found the book *Seedfolks* to be exciting and informative, filled with possibilities for engaging students in an integrated learning experience. The author weaves together the building of community with the planting of a communal garden. Birth and rebirth are evident as people become acquainted, and as seeds germinate and plants grow. *Seedfolks* offers many opportunities for building a cooperative classroom community (Slavin, 1995), and developing critical thinking (Beyer, 1988; Kneedler, 1985). Throughout the integrated lesson, students learn about themselves and each other as they compare and contrast characters and engage in problem solving. Shari, Dena, and Louise make use of a Double Diamond (Farris, 1997) as an alternative to the familiar Venn diagram for comparing and contrasting. The teachers engage the students in thinking aloud to model their thought processes. They employ active involvement and integrate the language arts with content areas such as geography, math, and science.

Getting Acquainted

Dena leads the group in introductions, asking each student in the class to tell something unique about his family, his life, or his past expe-

riences. She then introduces the book, *Seedfolks*, explaining how people
of various ages, from many different locations in the world, and with
unique experiences come to interact with each other because they live
in close proximity in a large city. The unifying element is a community
garden. She explains that each chapter in this short book tells about one
of the characters. She will read one or two chapters a day. Meanwhile,
students will begin engaging in related activities.

Comparing and Contrasting

Dena reads the first two chapters, after which she engages the students in a discussion about the characters' similarities and differences
using a Double Diamond (see Figure 5.4). She has made two diamond
shapes with masking tape on the floor, with a 3–foot space between
them. She has placed the name Kim in one diamond and the name Ana
in the other diamond. Each student who can state a characteristic that

Figure 5.4
Double Diamond

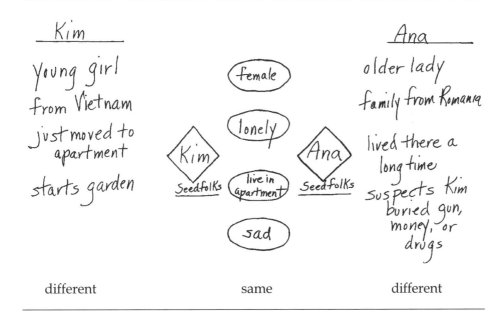

the characters have in common is asked to stand in the space between the diamonds. Each student who can state a unique characteristic of either Kim or Ana is asked to stand to the far side of the diamond bearing that character's name. At the conclusion of this activity, the point is obvious: People have differences and similarities, which is what makes them unique. Students then work in groups to complete a Double Diamond on paper to see which group can list the most common and the most unique characteristics of the two characters.

Seed Work — Categorization

Shari has obtained seed packets of 10 different kinds of seeds. She has cut the packets in half like a puzzle, taping the bottom half so as not to spill the seeds, resulting in 2 half-packages for each kind of seed. She places the half–packages into a hat and invites the 20 class members to take a piece of the puzzle. Students then have to find the person with the match to their piece. They will form "seed pairs." She invites the students to place their packets in one of three categories for which she has placed a label on a table: Perennials, Vegetables, and Annuals. Later students will be invited to research unique characteristics of their category.

Mathematics: Estimating and Problem Solving

Once all the packet pieces have been matched and placed in their categories, Louise focuses the discussion on math. The students will work in the seed pairs that were formed by matching the packages. She invites each pair to open their seed packets and pour the seeds into a plastic bag, attaching the bag to the two joined puzzle pieces. Students are asked to estimate how many seeds are in their bags. She invites the students to state their estimates to the group and to support their predictions by thinking aloud (Vacca, Vacca, & Gove, 2000). As students finish, Louise appoints one of each pair to count the seeds in their bag and give her the number. Each pair then tells the group how their estimates compare with the actual number of seeds in their packet and their theory about why their estimate was higher or lower.

Science: Planning for Planting

Dena reminds the students of the different characteristics of the characters in the book and draws the connection to differences in the seeds. She explains how those differences relate to planting information: when to plant, how to plant, how far seeds must be spaced, and the amount of sunlight and moisture the seeds need. She informs the class that this relates to climate, which relates to geography. She invites each pair of students to study their seed packets and mark a date on the school calendar when they should plant their seeds. She will be sure to have a small tray and soil for each student to plant and begin to nurture their seeds on the appointed day. Over the next few weeks students will study how to grow plants from seeds and will hear from some farmers and greenhouse operators who live outside the city. Students may revise their planting dates as they read, discuss, and hear experts give advice.

Geography: Location, Estimation, and Research

Shari has an inflatable globe for the students to locate the places from which the characters in *Seedfolks* have come. She invites students to sit in a circle while she reviews the chapters and the characters. When she names a character, she invites a student to volunteer to locate on the globe and demonstrate to the class where the character is from. The globe is tossed to that student, who holds it until Shari names another character. The globe is passed to another student who volunteers to locate that character's place of origin.

At the conclusion of this activity, Shari has the class predict whether they think there are many growing places on the globe. "Let's estimate how many places on the globe are good for growing. Notice the alliteration: g-g-g—good growing places on the globe," she says, unable to resist a teachable moment. "What percent of the world do you think is suitable for growing the flowers or vegetables from our packets? In your pairs, write down a percentage, and then we'll play a game to make another kind of estimate."

Once students have estimated a percentage of the earth suitable for growing their plants and vegetables, Shari explains the game. "I'll throw this globe to someone. Wherever your thumb lands when you catch it, we'll record that location and get a group consensus on whether our plants and vegetables could grow there. Then you'll throw it to someone else and we'll do the same. When we finish, we'll total the number of places we found and our opinions of whether something could grow there. We'll convert our numbers to percentages and you can compare them to the percentages you estimated."

After the students have had their thumbs recorded for landing on continents, oceans, and the Arctic and Antarctic Circles, Shari assigns locations for each pair to research. First, they study recommended growing conditions and climate on their seed packages. Then they use the library encyclopedias or the Internet to find out about growing conditions in one of the "thumb" locations (excluding oceans). When the class reconvenes, they are surprised at the limited percentage of the Earth's surface that is suitable for growing their plants and vegetables. They also make recommendations from their research as to where their plants and vegetables could grow.

Science: Writing and Illustrating

Dena presents the class with lima beans she has soaked in moist towels. She hands one to each pair and invites the students to identify the three parts: embryo, seed coat, and food storage. Then she hands each pair of students a peanut in a shell, shows them how to open it carefully, and asks them to look for the same three parts. Students are surprised to discover the same three parts in the peanut. They discuss the similarities and differences among the lima beans and peanuts. Tomorrow, she tells them, they will be given a diagram of a seed (see Figure 5.5) and asked to label the three parts from memory.

She engages the students in discussing how people have an outer shell and an inner self that affect them. She invites students to write about how their outer shell looks and how their inner self feels. She reads from her own journal to encourage them. She invites them to draw pictures of their outer shells and inner selves. She then invites the students to come up with a moral or lesson we can learn from *Seedfolks*. Students giggle and think it is obvious.

Figure 5.5
Parts of a Seed

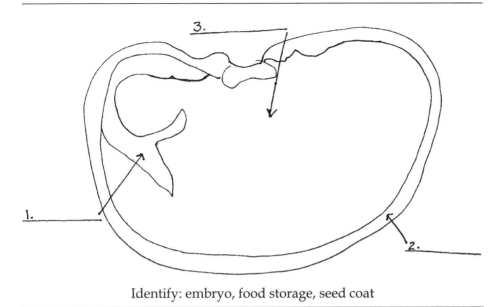

Identify: embryo, food storage, seed coat

"Good," says Dena. "That's what I hoped! In your seed pairs, write in your journals what you learned from *Seedfolks* and then we'll share it with the class. You see, even though we all probably learned a similar lesson, we may each construct the meaning a bit differently. I'll also write in my journal what I learned and share it with you. If anyone else wants to share about your outer shell and inner self, we can do that tomorrow. However, you may keep this private if you wish."

Summary

Shari, Dena, and Louise have provided an integrated language arts experience in which students experience efferent and aesthetic response (Rosenblatt, 1985) to plants and people. They inspired interest and obtained active involvement. From here they could have students select an ethnic group to research and present to the class. Further study and research on scientific aspects of planting are limitless. They have introduced their students to a broad literacy adventure.

Children's Book Cited

Fleischman, P. (1997). *Seedfolks*. New York: HarperCollins.

Related Children's Books

Seeds

Carle, E. (1990). *The tiny seed*. New York: Simon & Schuster.

Cole, J. (1995). *The magic school bus plants seeds: A book about how things grow*. New York: Scholastic.

Gibbons, G. (1993). *From seed to plant*. New York: Holiday House.

Harpern, S. (1998). *The surprise garden*. New York: Scholastic.

Jordon, H.J. (1992). *How a seed grows*. New York: HarperCollins.

Marzollo, J. (1996). *I'm a seed*. New York: Scholastic.

People

Spier, P. (1988). *People*. New York: Doubleday.

Neighborhoods

Ancona, G. (1998). *Jose's neighborhood*. San Diego, CA: Harcourt Brace.

Hughes, S. (1997). *Tales of Trotter Street*. Cambridge, MA: Candlewick Press.

Hyppolite, J. (1999). *Ola shakes it up*. New York: Bantam Doubleday.

Krull, K. (1996). *The other side: How kids live in a California Latino neighborhood*. New York: Penguin Putnam.

Medearis, A.S. (1997). *Rum–A–Tum*. New York: Holiday House.

Medoff, P. (1998). *Streets of hope*. Cambridge, MA: South End Press.

Quattlebaum, M. (1996). *A year on my street*. New York: Dell.

Soto, G. (1994). *Neighborhood odes*. New York: Scholastic Books. (Poems describing the cultural life of a Mexican American neighborhood.)

STUDY OPPOSITES WITH *TOPS AND BOTTOMS*

(Adapted and illustrated by Janet Stevens)

To get food for his family, hare makes a deal with lazy bear. A delightful tale shows how clever hare is as he tricks bear and harvests crops while bear sleeps through it all.

Children's Choices for 1996. Reprinted from *The Reading Teacher*, October 1996.

 Activities for This Book

Vocabulary
Brainstorming antonyms
Predicting story from cover
Reading aloud by teacher
Discussion of illustrations and theme
Forming trios
Choosing top, bottom, and middle of story

Collaborating on introduction and conclusion
Illustrating the text
Publishing the books
Sharing
Reading to younger grades
Reading to family

Karen De Young, a teacher in a small rural school, enjoys sharing picture books with her middle school students. She believes that the full potential of picture books is not realized when they are used only for younger children. Middle school students are able to see, hear, and experience a deeper range of nuances than younger students can. Karen's reading and writing projects for her middle school students begin with an exposure to a picture book. The real benefits can be seen in the students' interest in further exploration and reading and their enthusiasm for publishing and sharing.

The majority of families connected with the school are two–parent families with both parents working in a nearby city. There are also a significant number of farm families. The families support the school and want a good education for their children. They encourage them to read and to do well in school. Many of the families do not have the newspaper delivered to their home on a regular basis but do subscribe to a variety of magazines. They also frequently visit the local public library.

Karen helps her middle schoolers broaden and deepen their appreciation for picture books. She invites them to examine the coordination of text and illustrations. She finds *Tops and Bottoms* to be an excellent example of "how an illustrator has chosen to convey meaning through certain elements of art, principles of composition, and other factors relating to picture book design" (Keifer, 1995, p. 193).

The following project contains some unique features: using a picture book with middle schoolers, broadening the understanding of antonyms, and sharing published books with students in younger grades.

Vocabulary

Karen does a lot of work on vocabulary development with her middle school students. She knows the key role vocabulary plays in high school content area reading. In working with antonyms she looks for strategies that challenge her students to work with antonyms in a variety of print contexts.

In preparing her students for making *Tops and Bottoms* books of their own, Karen chooses a spelling–vocabulary lesson in which the students build lists of antonyms. By brainstorming with each other, the students excitedly come up with so many antonyms that the chalkboard is full.

Karen ends the lesson with a brief comment: "You wouldn't believe what some people do with antonyms! We will talk about that tomorrow!" The students are intrigued and eager to continue their study of opposites.

Reading

The next day, Karen and her students sit on the floor in the reading corner to review the antonym list from the previous day. Karen introduces the book *Tops and Bottoms* pointing out the bear and rabbit on the cover. She asks, "What might a rabbit and a bear have to do with tops and bottoms?"

Students eagerly predict possibilities.

"The bear eats the rabbit!" suggests Joe.

"Gross," exclaims Kim, "I think they're friends!"

"What about 'tops and bottoms'?" Karen reminds them.

"Maybe they 'morph' into each other, you know, the top of the rabbit and the bottom of the bear!" suggests Kevin.

"Let's read and find out," responds Karen before the wild ideas proliferate.

Karen reads the book to the students, making sure each student can see the pictures as she reads. She encourages the students to comment on what they see in the pictures as the reading continues.

When the first read–through is finished, Karen goes back to the beginning and shows the sequence of pictures again, noting the details in each one. For example, in the picture that shows the inside of the rabbit hole, the illustrator has used a variety of recycled materials, including the plastic rings from a six–pack of soda as the ladder to the exit. "What might the rabbit's unusual ladder show about its view of life?" she asks, and the students respond,

"He's cheap!"

"He's poor!"

"He's environmentally aware!"

The students look for the variety of ways the illustrator shows the difference between the philosophy of life of the bear and the rabbit, which is manifested in how they live.

Writing

Karen then introduces the connected writing project, an Opposites Book to share with the elementary classes (see Figure 5.6, page 164). Placing the students in groups of three, she encourages each trio to pick a pair of antonyms (opposites) for which they will be able to find a middle, just as the rabbit found corn to be a middle crop for the leaf crops and the root crops. The will build their stories around the pair of opposites they have chosen. This aspect of antonyms raises the complexity

Figure 5.6
Opposites Books

Tops and Bottoms
by Janet Stevens

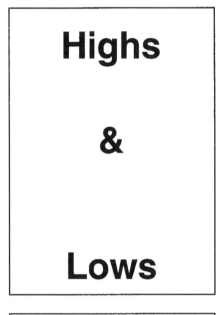

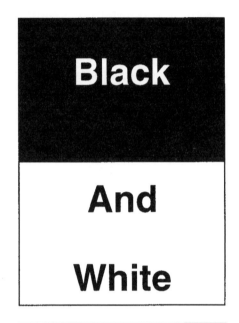

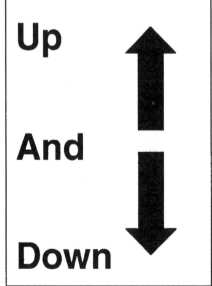

of thought from previous antonym work in earlier grades. The students work from the lists of antonyms they had built the previous day. Once the trios have picked their antonyms, Karen directs them to discuss and decide on the direction the story will go. Karen reminds the students of the artwork and its importance to the story, for that, too, plays an important part in the story's direction. "Write what you will be able to illustrate," she reminds the class.

Students engage in the writing process including prewriting, writing or drafting, and rewriting, but in a cooperative learning format (Slavin, 1995). The trios brainstorm characters, a problem, events, and a solution to their stories. Each trio then decides who will write which part of the story, equivalent to top, bottom, and middle. Each student writes a first draft of his or her part of the trio's story, consulting with others as necessary. After the first drafts are completed, the trio works together on the wording of the introductory and the concluding parts of the story. Then they read over the entire story, editing and making revisions as needed.

Art

The next step involves drawing the pictures to go with the story. Placing the pictures is important, Karen tells the groups, adding, "The younger students you read to may not be able to or willing to follow the words on the page. Your pictures have to tie in with the story and have enough details to keep the eyes busy while the ears hear the words." Students learn about the coordination of text and illustration as they publish their books. The writing process continues over several days. Finally, illustrations and word processing are completed and the covers are attached to the Opposites Books inspired by *Tops and Bottoms*. Karen binds the books for the students and makes arrangements for sharing their books with elementary classes.

Sharing

Many of the middle school students have younger siblings in the elementary classes, which provides an added incentive to make a wonderful project: They will be able to share the book with a family member in school. Finally, the students take their books home to share with their families, supplying another admiring audience who gives heart-warming praise.

Summary

Speaking, listening, reading, and writing, the key elements of literacy, have occurred over a succession of days. Students have listened, brainstormed, created, and shared words. Literacy has taken place on many levels in this project. Students have thought deeply about the meaning of a book and the author's intended message while experiencing the coordination of text and illustrations as they created their own books. They have worked collaboratively in trios and experienced the joy of sharing with diverse audiences. Karen concludes, "The students have a deep satisfaction in their completed projects and the enthusiastic responses they received from their listeners."

Children's Book Cited

Stevens, J. (1995). *Tops and bottoms*. San Diego, CA: Harcourt Brace.

Related Children's Books

Gordon, M. (1991). *Lift and learn opposites*. Upper Saddle River, NJ: Silver Burdett Press.

Inkpen, M. (1995). *Kipper's book of opposites*. San Diego, CA: Harcourt Brace.

Mabie, G. (1991). *A picture book of animal opposites*. Mahwah, NJ: Troll Communications L.L.C.

Murphy, C. (1998). *Chuck Murphy's black cat, white cat: A pop–up book of opposites*. New York: Simon & Schuster.

Potter, K.R. (1999). *This and that: A book of opposites*. San Francisco: Chronicle Books.

Scarry, R. (1999). *Mr. Fixit's opposites*. New York: Simon & Schuster.

Schroeder, P.J.P. (1996). *Opposites*. Vero Beach, FL: Rourke Publishing.

Stower, A. (Ill.). (1998). *Opposites*. Austin, TX: Raintree Steck–Vaughn.

DRAGONWINGS
by Laurence Yep

Dare to Dream With *Dragonwings*

(by Laurence Yep)

Well researched historical novel set in early 20th century San Francisco Chinatown, giving vivid details of Chinese folklore, racial relationships, the 1906 earthquake, and a fictionalized account of a Chinese man who built a flying machine with help from the Wright brothers. Excellent discussion material countering Chinese American stereotypes. IRA 1976 Children's Book Award.

Classroom Choices: Children's Trade Books 1975. Reprinted from *The Reading Teacher*, October 1976.

 Activities for This Book

Free-writing exercise

Discussing Chinese culture

How names are formed

Directed Reading Activity (modified)

Vocabulary preparation

Set motivation

Purpose for reading

Question–Answer Relationships

Compare and contrast

Discussion and reflection

Story map

Word map

Letter writing

Oral presentations

Construct kites

Assemble model airplanes

Make dream catchers

Extension activities

Gretchen Ziegler shares *Dragonwings* with her sixth–grade students in a culturally diverse suburb of a large midwestern city. Her class is a diverse mix of students from other countries and from second-generation families with at least one parent who immigrated. There is also a diversity of races and ethnic backgrounds among her students who were born in the United States. Some of the students use English as their second language and, therefore, the story seems appropriate for her class. She believes that story content that is culturally familiar will aid the comprehension of many of her students (Nurss & Hough, 1992). She also believes that students can generalize and find similarities between the experiences of the Chinese immigrants in *Dragonwings* and their own experiences. Her class also has students originating from Latin America, the Caribbean, and African countries. She knows that these students will be able to identify with the feelings of cultural difference experienced by the characters in the book.

Gretchen sees value in developing sensitivity to diverse cultures among those students in her class who were born and raised in the United States. She sees some evidence that her students' make disparaging remarks about differences in classmates, and she has heard the unkind comments about clothing, mannerisms, speech, and food that some students have directed at others. Although she realizes that middle school children can be unkind, and even cruel, she is determined to do her best to change this situation in her classroom. She believes that children's literature is a powerful stimulus to develop sensitivity and appreciation for other cultures. She hopes that her students will identify with Moon Shadow in the story, and that they will get "inside his skin" and begin asking themselves, "How would I feel if I were Moon Shadow?"

Inspired by the actual life of a Chinese immigrant who made a "flying machine" in 1909, *Dragonwings* is a powerful story about a young Chinese boy, Moon Shadow, who sails from China to California in the early 1900s to work with his father, whom he has never met. Moon Shadow has lived with his mother in China all his life. His father left for the United States before he was born in order to send money to the family and, hopefully, bring them to the United States some day. An uncle, who lived in the United States and then returned to China, takes Moon Shadow on the long journey to live with his father. Although his mother is reluctant to see him go, Moon Shadow accedes to his father's wish that he come.

Moon Shadow and his father, Windrider, face many obstacles as they try to carry out their dreams. Some of these include living in poverty, enduring strenuous labor, experiencing a San Francisco earthquake, and longing for home and family. Moon Shadow grows, learning to respect and admire his father, while Windrider learns about the patience and responsibility needed to be a father to a young boy. Both discover that becoming a family is the most important thing.

Introducing the Book

Gretchen introduces the students to *Dragonwings* by having them do a short free–write on what their feelings would be if, for some reason, they found themselves in a new and different country far away from home; for students who actually had this experience in coming to the United States, she encourages them to write about their true feelings. She asks them to express their excitement and concern about the problems they would face, or did face, in this new situation. She provides some questions to stimulate their thinking:

What are your impressions of this new city or country?

Describe how the people look to you.

How do the school environment and the subjects students learn compare with your education in the place you emigrated from?

Immediately, Gretchen sees a teachable moment: "Let's talk about two similar words: *immigrate* and *emigrate*. First of all, can anyone think of words that come from these root, or base, words?" Students suggest the words *immigrant* and *immigrated*. They wonder if there are similar words for *emigrate*, like *emigrant* and *emigrated*. Once the definition has been read and the terms discussed, the students see that an immigrant is someone who comes into another country, while an emigrant is someone who leaves a country. They decide that a person can be both. Gretchen tells the students that Moon Shadow, whom they are about to meet, is an emigrant from China and an immigrant to the United States. Because of her students' age, the issue of fitting in is a significant one, and Gretchen thinks they will easily imagine how they would feel in a foreign place.

Following this activity Gretchen attempts to draw on the students' knowledge of the culture and the traditions of the Chinese people. As part of this discussion, she explains the importance of names and invites her students to reverse their names, putting their last name first followed by their first name, in the style of the Chinese. Sixth grader Jill Jones becomes Jones Jill, and John Lee became Lee John, which was already familiar to him because of his Asian origins. Gretchen then discusses the fact that traditionally, as they grew up, the Chinese are often given a third name that describes what they did or what kind of person they were. The students then select a third name for themselves and explain why they selected it. Jill decides to be Jones Jill Helpful Friend, and John selects Lee John Expert Kite Flier. Students readily offer suggestions when their classmates are reluctant to identify their qualities or talents. Gretchen tells the students to think of qualities or talents they admire in the person sitting next to them and to tell that person. She has already begun to work on a theme of developing appreciation for others. Students share their free–writes in small groups along with the names they have given themselves.

Using Directed Reading Activity

Gretchen gives a short book talk on the historical setting and significance of the era in which the story occurs: in the early 1900s on the West Coast when Asian immigrants began arriving in major cities, particularly in California, and settled into their own areas within the cities. The majority of the early Asian immigrants were Chinese. Gretchen mentions Chinatown, a name given to sections of several large cities in the United States where Chinese people settled. The students are eager to begin reading and read the first three chapters silently. Gretchen feels it is important for the students to understand the relationship between the Chinese and the Americans, and she asks them to read with this purpose in mind.

Throughout the reading of the book, Gretchen uses a modified form of the Directed Reading Activity (DRA) (Vacca, Vacca, & Gove, 2000):

- introducing vocabulary
- motivating or enticing students to read by giving a bit of information
- setting a purpose for reading: "We are reading to find out…"
- guiding comprehension with questions

These four aspects of the DRA are components of most of Gretchen's reading lessons as she guides her students' literacy development. She generally selects a few chapters a day. She works hard to make sure her questions are not just the literal factual level and forms her questions around the QAR strategy (Raphael, 1986), which deepens the students' comprehension of the material by making them recognize different sources of information. QAR seems particularly appropriate for this story because so much of the children's comprehension requires them to do higher level thinking. As presented by Vacca, Vacca, and Gove (2000), QAR uses the following types of questions:

Right There—The answer is in the text.

Think and Search—The answer is in the text or pictures, but you may have to do some searching and figuring out.

In My Head—The questions include On My Own and Author and You.

> On My Own—The answer is in your head, but the story got you thinking about your knowledge.

> Author and You—This answer is not in the story. Use your own knowledge and what you read about to come up with the answer.

Following their silent reading, Gretchen prompts the students with three Think-and-Search questions. The students know immediately that they will have to search the text and read between the lines to find the answers:

Why did the Chinese think that the Americans were demons?

Why did the Chinese feel threatened by the Americans, just as the Americans felt threatened by the Chinese?

A lively discussion results as students and teacher sort through the facts and the unfortunate incidents that occurred between the groups. They look at the myths that each group believes about the other, the sources of these beliefs, and the resulting prejudices that developed.

After the class has read the book in its entirety, Gretchen has the students compare and contrast life in California during Moon Shadow and Windrider's time with life in the United States as we know it today. Students work in pairs and record their findings on a chart that shows life in California in the early 20th century, and life in the United States to-day, and similarities between then and now (see Figure 5.7).

This activity is followed by a discussion that centers around family. Gretchen announces some In–My–Head questions for discussion and reflection to be followed by a writing activity:

How might it feel to be an ocean away from your family?

What would it be like to meet your father for the first time when you are 8 years old and moving to a strange country?

Why do you think it was so important to Moon Shadow that he please his father?

Is there someone in your life that you look up to or someone you feel it is important to have him or her think well of you?

What are your dreams? And what are you willing to do to make them come true?

Writing Activities

Several different writing activities engage the children in extending their understanding, and these activities relate back to their comprehension of the story. Gretchen first asks them to think on the Right-There level, capturing the facts by filling in a story map (see Figure 5.8, page 174). While mapping story elements (Stein & Glenn, 1979, 1982) has been used extensively in elementary schools, particularly the lower grades, Gretchen uses story mapping with her sixth graders for two reasons: The maps capture the major elements of the story in a summary–outline form, and students must begin with the facts from which to extend their learning. The students work in small groups to produce the major elements of the story. Because a limited number of events can be included on one story map, each group highlights different events based on those that group members found most poignant. Each member shares an important event, and the group sequences them in chronological order to complete the events section of the map.

Gretchen sees another opportunity to work on comprehension, to develop vocabulary, and to include a bit of writing. She labels this activity a Think and Search Activity. Because many themes are woven

Figure 5.7
Comparison Chart for Life in the United States

Dragonwings
by Laurence Yep

Difference	Same	Difference
The early 20th century	people can be mean	The early 21st century
horse and wagon the "demons" (white people) won't let Moon Shadow go to their schools Wright brothers making first airplane. demon tests dirigible (blimp) to race it flying kites was exciting	Kids make fun of each other - like Jack teases Moon Shadow Kids do not understand each other because of differences - like Robin and Moon Shadow at first there are kind people like Miss Whitlaw Sometimes gruff people are really nice underneath - like uncle Earthquakes still happen.	cars, trucks, vans, SUVs all kids can go to public schools thousands of airplanes fly every day blimps only used to fly above sports events flying kites can be a sport to compete in, but most kids want more exciting things to do.

Figure 5.8
Story Map

Dragonwings
by Laurence Yep

Setting:
Where: San Francisco, CA
When: 1903

Characters —— Who: Moon Shadow, his father, Windrider, Uncle and the company of relatives, Miss Whitlaw, Robin

Problem or Goal: Windrider wants to be a dragon and build a flying machine. He sees this as a test.

Beginning Event: Moon Shadow sails from China to San Francisco, CA to live with his father

Events: Father and son work in the company's laundry.

Father and son leave after a fight to rescue Black Dog, Uncle's son.

Father and son live in a stable and become friends with Miss Whitlaw and Robin.

Father builds kites.

Son corresponds with the Wright Brothers.

The earthquake hits.

Father and son move to Oakland and build a flying machine.

Resolution: Father realizes that there is more to being a dragon than flying.

He will rejoin the company and send for Mother to come from China.

Adapted from Stein & Glenn, 1979, 1982; Vacca, Vacca, & Gove, 2000.

throughout this book, Gretchen calls the students' attention to themes through a type of semantic mapping or webbing, which she calls Word Webbing. Each student chooses one of the themes from the story, such as family, perseverance, diligence, patience, kindness, tolerance, or another of their choosing. They complete the web by naming incidents in the story that depict that theme and citing page numbers as sources of evidence (see Figure 5.9, page 176). This web occurs following the reading of the book and requires students to review their reading, looking back to find answers they believe support their theme.

A more extensive writing activity is patterned after Moon Shadow's letter to the Wright Brothers, telling them of his dream to create a flying machine and seeking their direction as he and his father work on theirs. Gretchen works with the students to write letters to people whose area of expertise they want to know more about. They may ask the experts for information on an invention or discovery from the past or an invention or discovery they would like to see for the future. The sixth graders' letters may be sent or unsent, meaning they can actually be to a living person, or they can be a letter to someone they would like to question but cannot. "You'll write about what you would ask them if you could," Gretchen says.

Students who write to real people will send their letters and await a reply. The class brainstorms possible people to whom they could write. They also seek advice from a science professor at a nearby university who offers names of current inventors and scientists. The students also will do research on the people to whom they write and on their work in order to find out more about them, in case the person does not answer.

The unsent letters are handled in two ways. The students may do research themselves to find the answers, or they can trade letters with a classmate. If they trade, each will become the other's expert, posing as the person to whom the letter was written and doing research to answer each other's letter. Pairs confer with each other to clarify the contents of the letter and to seek further information.

Books, magazines, newspapers, and the Internet provide information. At the beginning of this project, students share their letters with the whole class so that they all have an idea about what their classmates are doing. Gretchen plans to hold weekly update sessions in which students report briefly on their progress and ask for help where needed. For the oral presentations they will eventually give, the students have several options from which to choose. They may act as if they were the person to whom the letter was directed, dressing as the character and

Figure 5.9
Word Web

Dragonwings
by Laurence Yep

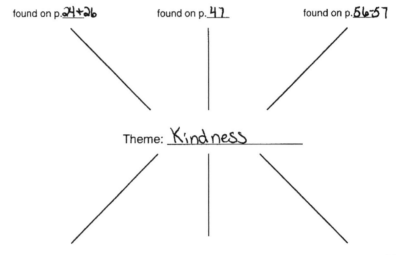

Father, Uncle, and the relatives in the Company welcome MoonShadow with a feast and gifts.

found on p. 24+26

Uncle makes a wooden carving of Monkey for MoonShadow

found on p. 47

Father helps a "demon" (the Chinese word for white people) start his car.

found on p. 56-57

Theme: Kindness

Father rescues Black Dog.

found on p. 73-75

Miss Whitlaw shows many Kindnesses to MoonShadow+Windrider.

serves milk + cookies
found on p. 108-11

Shows interest in dragons
found on pp. 114-118

helps him write letter to Wright brothers
found on pp. 129-130

summons the company to help Windrider
found on pp. 234-235

Uncle loans Windrider the money to buy a share into the company.

found on p. 243

bringing props to enhance their presentations. They may form their presentation as a monologue in the first person, such as, "I, Alexander Graham Bell…." Or, they may be a news reporter reporting in the third person, "This is (name) for Channel 1 News, reporting to you on an amazing invention…." The oral presentations will follow their writing and research after sufficient time has been given for preparation.

Art Projects

As a culmination to the study of *Dragonwings*, Gretchen introduces three art projects from which the students will choose one. For any project, they may work alone or with a partner. Most choose to work with someone else because the projects are challenging and time consuming. The first project is kite making. Students will design and construct kites and include symbols pertinent to the Chinese culture or to the story of *Dragonwings*. Some of the students who undertake this project consult with local Asian Americans, often relatives of students from the class, to ask for symbols for the words they want on their kites. They make the kites by constructing wooden frames and covering the frames with layers of colorful tissue paper. On the top layer they carefully write their symbols. A further requirement is that the kites be workable, that they will fly in a modest wind that will not tear the tissue paper. The highlight of the project occurs when students take the kites outdoors and fly them.

Another project the students can select is to construct a model airplane from a kit. The challenge in this project lies in following directions and in being faithful to detail. Once again, a requirement is that the plane actually can fly. Gretchen finds this task much easier said than done; it is amazing how heavy glue can become when it is applied by a sixth grader. Several students need to redo sections of their airplanes, removing and replacing glue, until they are light enough to fly. A moderately windy day is also the setting for the demonstration of model airplane flying.

The third project is to make a dreamcatcher, which appeals to the students because of their familiarity with dreamcatchers from reading Native American folklore and literature. (This connects to Windrider's faithfulness to his dream and Moon Shadow's sharing in his father's dream.) Connecting the Native American concept of catching dreams with the realization of Windrider's dream allows for noting similarities among diverse cultures. Students who choose this project will research dreamcatchers and create one to hang in the classroom.

Extension Activities

A logical extension occurs one day during share time when Samantha raises her hand.

"I really just want to say something. I worked on a dreamcatcher and that made me think about dreams. I think we all have dreams and our dreams differ from each other," Samantha says.

"Yes!" replies Jermaine as he high–fives his neighbor. "Exactly what Martin Luther King, Jr., talked about in his speech, 'I Have a Dream.' Don't we have that book around here?"

"Yes. You may get it from the Book Nook," says Gretchen. "You're giving me an idea. I'll ask our school media specialist as well as our local librarian if they can come up with a collection of books that tell about people's dreams and visions. How does that sound?"

"Great. And then can we make our own?" asks Sari.

"We could even create a Dreams book!" exclaims Jerry.

"More writing? Oh, no!" counters Jermaine. "Forget I ever said something."

"Well, it doesn't have to begin as a big project, especially since we're still doing our other research," says Gretchen. "But the idea of dreams and hopes is too important to ignore."

She proposes a format to start with that extends a theme from *Dragonwings*, recognizes an interest that should be cultivated in her students, yet does not discourage them by requiring a large amount of work. She asks the students to fold a sheet of paper into three sections horizontally and write one sentence starter at the top of each section. She tells the class to think about these questions and fill them in sometime before share time next week:

I have a dream _____.

I could help this dream come true by _____ .

This dream could help others because _____.

Summary

Gretchen has used a classic novel whose subject is a universal struggle of people that all of us have felt at some time. We may not like change; we rebel against leaving a home, city, or country; we feel and act like outsiders. Sometimes we try to fit in, yet want to maintain individuality. Sometimes we deal with differences in peaceful and constructive ways. Other times we engage in meanness and even violence.

In a 21st century classroom, Gretchen uses a 25–year–old book to show students how similar many of our character traits are today, how some of the same human struggles exist, and how we can identify with literary characters as we engage in literacy activities. She engages her students in excellent literacy instruction, taking the best from the Directed Reading Activity, and incorporating contemporary ideas and strategies. She guides the students' reading and works on all levels of comprehension. She includes writing at several points and has both short and long assignments. Her art projects connect to the story and beyond as seen by the students' reactions. Their discussion toward the end of the project turns into literacy activities that could develop into more literacy learning.

Gretchen's teaching reflects integrated language arts, a direction in literacy instruction that will continue in the 21st century. She embodies universal themes with a book written in the early years of the Children's Choices project and connects it with current literacy practices.

Children's Books Cited

King, M.L., Jr. (1999). *I have a dream*. New York: Scholastic. (Original speech presented in 1963)

Yep, L. (1975). *Dragonwings*. New York: HarperCollins.

Other Books by Laurence Yep

American dragons. (1993). New York: HarperCollins.

The case of the Goblin People. (1997). New York: HarperCollins.
The case of the Lion Dance. (1999). New York: HarperCollins.
The cook's family. (1998). New York: Putnam.
Dragon cauldron. (1991). New York: HarperCollins.
The dragon prince. (1996). New York: HarperCollins.
Dragon war. (1992). New York: HarperCollins.
The journal of Wong Ming–Chung: A Chinese miner. (2000). New York: Scholastic.
Later, Gator. (1995). New York: Hyperion Books.
The lost garden. (1991). (Autobiography) New York: Simon & Schuster.
Mountain light. (1985). New York: HarperCollins.
Ribbons. (1996). New York: Putnam.
The serpent's children. (1984). New York: HarperCollins.

Use Jean Fritz Books to Enhance a Unit on the American Revolution and Colonial America

Eight future teachers asked if they could teach a lesson to a group of students in preparation for their upcoming student teaching experience. They wanted to return to the school where they had worked assessing reading and writing with individual students. The fifth-grade teacher, Erin Mulhall, agreed and suggested that they base their lessons on historical biographies by Jean Fritz that had been introduced to the class to enhance their study of the American Revolution and Colonial America. The selected award-winning books were relevant to the theme and provided appropriate reading levels for the students involved: *George Washington's Mother*; the *School Library Journal* Best Book of the Year, *Can't You Make Them Behave, King George?*; *The New York Times* Outstanding Book of the Year, *What's the Big Idea, Ben Franklin?*; and the *Boston Globe-Hornbook* Award Honor Book, *Will You Sign Here, John Hancock?*

The future teachers were enthusiastic about planning lessons around the Jean Fritz books. They knew she made history come alive by relating humorous and interesting facts about historical characters. Furthermore, many of her historical biographies have been recognized as Notable Social Studies Trade Books for young people by a joint project of the National Council for Social Studies and CBC. The future teachers also knew that each of the chosen books had appeared on the Children's Choices booklists.

Although the books had been placed in different age categories by the Children's Choices teams, they felt that the four books coordinated well with the theme. *George Washington's Mother* had been placed in the Younger Reader category, but seemed suited to a group of children who were reading at a lower level than their fifth–grade classmates. *What's the Big Idea, Ben Franklin?* and *Will You Sign Here, John Hancock?* came from the Intermediate category. *Can't You Make Them Behave, King George?* had been placed in the Informational Books category, a designation used by Children's Choices teams in some years the list was produced.

The future teachers investigated how Jean Fritz may have invented some of the actual conversations and inner thoughts of the characters of her books. They discussed how an author of historical biographies will remain true to major events, while conceiving of how parts of the story actually played out. They concluded that her style of writing contributed to the interest her books generated among children across age, grade, and reading levels. As they looked forward to planning with a peer, they also anticipated sharing their lessons and evaluating the lessons following the actual teaching.

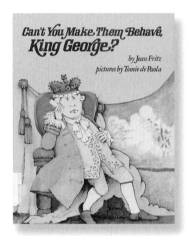

CAN'T YOU MAKE THEM BEHAVE, KING GEORGE?
(by Jean Fritz, ill. by Tomie dePaola)

The American Revolution takes on a new, human, and humorous dimension with this characterization of King George the Third, presented with all his foibles and idiosyncrasies. Children in primary and middle grades enjoy the humorous text and illustrations. Recommended as an addition to the social studies collection.

Classroom Choices for 1978. Reprinted from *The Reading Teacher*, October 1978.

Background Knowledge	Ideas for arguments
K–W–L	Noting our ideas
Relating title to book content	Paragraphs to support ideas
Reading aloud by teachers	Summarizing in one sentence
Answering W (What I Want to Know) questions	Advancing an argument
	Town Message Board
Supporting answers by rereading from the text	Posting arguments
Brainstorming	Announcing a formal debate

The future teachers divided themselves into pairs, each pair planning a 40-minute lesson. Erin divided her fifth graders into four groups of seven or eight students each.

Kelly Kenyon and Meredith Woolman's group was not too excited about its unit on the American Revolution. But when the teacher presented books by Jean Fritz as an interesting way to get the facts by reading a good story, the fifth graders were eager to give the books a try.

Background Knowledge: K–W–L

Kelly and Meredith tap into the class's study of the American Revolution by beginning with a K–W–L activity (Ogle, 1986) on the chalkboard. They ask the students what they already know about King George and what the title of the book tells them. They do this orally because they only have 40 minutes and want to spend the bulk of their time on other activities. Students' answers are limited:

King George ruled England.

King George wanted to tax the colonies.

King George wanted to own the colonies.

Kelly asks what significance the title might have. It becomes apparent that the students are intrigued by the title. They know that the American colonies are rebelling against British rule and British taxation. They never thought of the problem in terms of behaving. The title has caught their interest, a common reaction of students to so many Jean Fritz books.

Having been drawn into the book by the title, the students have much that they want to learn. Their eagerness provides the perfect setting for the teachers to read a segment of the book aloud. The students are told to jot down the questions they want answered as they brainstorm aloud the W column of the K–W–L. Now, as the teachers take turns reading, the students listen for and write answers to their questions. Then they look in their books and find a sentence or a passage to support their answers. The fifth graders are eager to reread it because the teacher's reading aloud has made the text familiar.

A brief portion of the book is used during this lesson: two to four pages so students can easily review the pages to support their answers. They share with a partner what their question was, the answer they decided on, and the proof they found in the text.

The Great Debate

"Are you ready to take sides?" asks Meredith. "We need some British and some Americans!"

"Aw, who wants to be British? They're the bad guys!" responds Aaron.

"Well, for this activity we need both British and Americans. Besides, there are often two sides to every issue that comes up in life and this is good practice for us to be able to take different sides. Besides, oops, did you hear how I used 'sides' as part of another word? Let's put that down on our Word Wall for study sometime. Jamie, will you write *side* and *besides* on the Word Wall?" Kelly adds.

She continues, "Now, where was I? Oh, yes, I remember that on your state tests when you get to the next level you are asked to read several articles and discuss the different sides of an issue. This will be good practice for us here!"

"American," yells Nye–Nye.

"I'll be British—just for the sake of argument!" says Aaron.

"Yea, he likes to argue! You should hear him at lunch!" adds Jamie.

Meredith takes up the cause. "OK, we have one good sport: Aaron. Who else will be British?"

"Hey, he's not a good sport, but I'll be British, too," says Jamie.

The rest of the group decides: Emily, British; Chris, American; Lisa, American.

Advancing an Argument

"Now I want you to talk about your arguments," states Meredith.

The students meet in two groups—British and American—and brainstorm possible arguments. Each group appoints a scribe who takes notes. The notes are placed where each group member can see them for reference.

The next step involves having each student write a paragraph to support his or her side of the argument. They look at the brainstormed listing of notes made by their group and take whatever they want from it. Although each student has access to all the facts brainstormed by his or her side, each individual will produce a slightly different version of his or her argument.

After they complete the paragraphs, the students must take their argument and summarize it in one sentence. As each student gets a chance to speak for the British or American position, they get to "register" their one-sentence argument by putting it on a class poster titled "Both Sides of the Debate" (see Figure 5.10, page 186).

"The British go first. After all, they are the oldest. They existed before America," explains Kelly, who sees tension and excitement mounting on each side. As each student speaks, they place their argument on their side.

The students begin to sound like the town criers of Colonial America as they loudly proclaim,

"These taxes were fair because they were to benefit America!"

"We were mad at King George because we thought he was wasting our tax money on bad stuff!"

Figure 5.10
Both Sides of the Debate

Can't You Make Them Behave, King George?
by Jean Fritz

British	Arguments	American

British side:

I am the King we are taxing your

We the British fought a war for your benifit you will pay your share

These taxes were fair.

These taxes were fair because they were to benifit america.

The British who lived in America were still royal subjects of the king so they had the right to tax them.

American side:

We were mad at King George because we thought he was wasting are tax money on bad stuff. He was greed on money. I think we shouldn't pay taxes.

We've already spent money on the war. We don't want to spend anymore.

We don't want soldiers to live here. We can take care of ourself.

Town Message Board

The students are very excited now and eager to do more with what they learned, discussed, and wrote. They suggest a message board that replies to the following headlines:

Figure 5.11
Town Message Board: Pro-American Paragraph

Chris Boll

> We were made at King George
> because we want freedom. We don't
> want British troops in America. We
> dont want to be ruled by another
> country, we want to be a free country.
> We want to have our own goverment.
> We want to have our own religon.
> We want to have our own army

Should King George's subjects behave? Yes or No.
Read all about it on your town's announcement board today!

Under the headlines they place their written paragraphs and invite others to submit a paragraph taking either side of the issue. Pro–American (see Figure 5.11) and Pro–British paragraphs are posted. Notice is also given that a formal debate will take place at the end of the week. Participants are Aaron, Emily, and Jamie for the British side and Chris, Lisa, and Nye–Nye for the American side. The debate will take place next week, according to debating rules run by Kelly and Meredith, debate coaches.

Summary

Kelly and Meredith have taken a small amount of time they had with the students and parlayed it into a continuing lesson that builds excitement over time. They connected social studies with children's literature, enlivened the study of historical events, and introduced a popular author of informational and biographical material. They also have made meaningful connections to writing, speaking, and listening. Kelly and Meredith have gotten the students actively involved in studying issues and supporting a point of view, aspects of critical thinking. Together, with the three other Jean Fritz groups, they have contributed to a meaningful social studies–language arts connection in fifth grade.

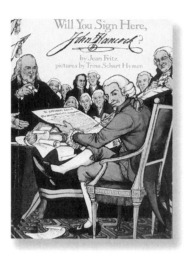

WILL YOU SIGN HERE, JOHN HANCOCK?

(by Jean Fritz, ill. by Trina Schart Hyman)

John Hancock's life and accomplishments are pictured in a human and humorous manner; children enjoy reading about the feats and failures of a famous person. This biography encourages further reading about other famous people.

Classroom Choices for 1977. Reprinted from *The Reading Teacher*, October 1977.

 Activities for This Book

Introducing the book	Sharing responses
"Reading" the cover	Biopoem format and example
Inferring the contents of the book	Writing biopoems
Reading and responding	Illustrating biopoems
Reading silently	Compose a class book
Writing impressions	

Beth Holtgeerts and Rachelle Brink decide to build a language arts lesson around *Will You Sign Here, John Hancock?* They think their fifth graders will be intrigued by the story of John Hancock and his large writing. Jean Fritz's description of him reveals a proud and privileged man. He was the first signer of the Declaration of Independence and a man who loved signing his name with great flourish. But there was a lot at stake, both literally and figuratively, with his signature.

> If America won the war, he would be honored as the first Signer; if America lost, he would be the first to be hanged for treason. John swished and swirled his curlicues. "There!" he said, "George the Third can read that without his spectacles. Now he can double the reward for my head." (Fritz, 1976, p. 30)

Introducing the Book

Beth and Rachelle ask the students what they know about John Hancock. When no one volunteers, they show the cover, and it becomes apparent that Hancock is signing something while others look on. In fact, the writing on the document he is signing says, "In Congress July 4, 1776, The unanimous Declaration of the thirteen States…."

"The Declaration of Independence," say several students.

"Oh, yea," responds Jerrad. "He's the guy with the big writing."

"Is that like 'big hair'?" asks Tiffany.

Jerrad isn't sure if she's joking or serious. He decides to answer honestly.

"I mean big signature," he explains.

"Right," replies Rachelle, "but there's a lot more to the story. I think we're ready to read the book."

Reading and Responding

Let's all read the first two pages silently, and then we'll talk about it," Rachelle suggests. After the group has finished, she asks them to write down their impressions of Hancock so far and share their responses with a neighbor. "Nice–looking, generous, kind, rich, friendly," are some of the responses.

The class continues in this way, reading silently, writing impressions, and talking about their responses. After completing a segment of the book, Beth takes over to ask some concluding questions:

What event sticks out in your head the most?

How do you feel about John?

What did you learn about John?

Writing Biopoems

"With all the information we now have about John Hancock , I'd like to introduce you to a biopoem," says Beth. She presents the form and gives an example using Abe Lincoln (see Figure 5.12). "If we get stuck, we can always look back in the book for more information, but I

Figure 5.12
Biopoem Form

Line 1: First name
Line 2: Four adjectives describing the person
Line 3: Sibling of (in our case, Enemy of...)
Line 4: Lover of
Line 5: Who feels (2 things)
Line 6: Who fears (2 things)
Line 7: Who would like to see
Line 8: Resident of
Line 9: Last name

Example- Abraham Lincoln

Abe
Honest, tall, bearded, thin
Husband of Mary
Lover of freedom, education, law
Who feels compassion, anger
Who fears war, death
Who would like to see the end of slavery
Resident of Washington D.C.
Lincoln

think you've already written and discussed a lot." She encourages the class. "How many of you think you can do one by yourself now?" she asks. All the hands go up. "Good," Beth exclaims, "and don't be afraid to leave a word blank if you get stuck. We'll help each other later when we've all written as much of the biopoem as we can."

Following individual composing of the biopoems students share them in groups (see Figure 5.13). They then illustrate their biopoems, visualizing the pictures of John Hancock they saw in the book and adding their own ideas of his appearance. A class book will be made containing each person's biopoem, and there is a possibility of later doing biopoems about several of the major figures of Colonial America.

Figure 5.13
Student Biopoem
John Hancock

Tiffany

John,
friendly, kind, generous, nice-looking
Enemy of King George
Lover of clothes and popularity
Who feels eager and anger
Who fears King George and of losing the
place of president
Who would like to see independence
Resident of Boston, Massachusetts
Hancock

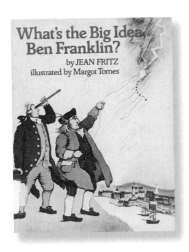

WHAT'S THE BIG IDEA, BEN FRANKLIN?

(by Jean Fritz, ill. By Margot Tomes)

Jean Fritz again presents a fine upper primary biography on an early American—Ben Franklin—and his many inventions. The author's detailed factual notes as well as the illustrator's accurate drawings of inventions stimulate further search for information about the man with a "twinkle in his eye and a new idea always in his mind."

Classroom Choices for 1977. Reprinted from *The Reading Teacher,* October 1997.

 Activities for This Book

Discussing static electricity	Conducting experiments
Reading and responding	Grammar attachment
Reading aloud by teachers	Sharing and suggesting further
Comprehending factually and	study
inferentially	

Kevin Sills and Jeralyn DeVries choose to combine a science lesson along with language arts and social studies. Using Fritz's retelling of the life of the big idea man, Ben Franklin, who was always inventing and experimenting, they choose to teach about electricity. A group demonstration of an experiment is followed by dividing the class into two smaller groups and allowing each to perform an experiment.

An Experimental Balloon

A balloon hangs from the ceiling with a face drawn on it. Jeralyn introduces it, "This is George and he has a terrible crush on me. I'm going to rub his face with wool. What do you think will happen?" She conducts an informal prediction session, patterned after a Directed

Listening–Thinking Activity (DLTA), a variation of Stauffer's (1975) Directed Reading–Thinking Activity (DRTA), but centered around observation and teacher explanation. The students offer hesitant answers:

"He'll break."

"Nothing."

"Show us!"

Jeralyn rubs George's face and steps away. She begins to circle the balloon, and it turns to face her with George's face following her circular movement.

"See?" she exclaims. "He has a crush on me! How did I make this happen?"

"It's the same thing when our clothes stick to us after we walk across a carpet," answers Jack. "My mom bought some kind of static stuff."

"Oh, yeah, we have that too," replies Grace. "It comes in a can and you spray it on your clothes to get rid of static electricity."

"Great! You've got the idea. Let's examine what happened with my friend, George," replies Jeralyn.

She then explains how George, the balloon, gained electrons when she rubbed it with wool. However, only the part of the balloon that was rubbed gained electrons and became negatively charged. It was attracted to her because she (or her hair) was positively charged. While the rest of the balloon remained neutrally charged, George's face followed the positively charged Jeralyn.

Reading and Responding

"Ben Franklin did much bigger and more dangerous experiments with electricity," she tells the class. "They helped him learn a lot, but I'm sure he'd advise us not to try them. Let's read an excerpt from the book together. Find the page with the bolt of lightning." The students eagerly find it. Jeralyn and Kevin read aloud as the students follow along. After the reading, they ask some questions and tell the class to read a sentence or portion of the text to support their answers. They decide to do the initial oral reading so as not to embarrass students by requiring them to read aloud, thus creating a reading performance situation (Vacca,

Vacca, & Gove, 2000). They would rather have the students hear the text and then read orally to support answers to comprehension questions.

What dangerous things did the early experimenters do? Find one or more sentences to support your answers.

How would you like to have been the boy suspended from the ceiling?

What advice would you give Ben Franklin about his electrical picnic experiment?

Electric Experiments

The class is eager to try their own experiments with electricity. Kevin divides the class into two groups, each of which will perform an experiment and report to the other group. Each group has four members who are given specific roles: leader, recorder, reporter, and organizer.

Experiment I

The organizer passes out an inflated balloon to each student in the group. The leader is given a piece of wool and a spoon on a string to hang from the ceiling. Each group member is given one of the following objects: a comb, scarf, ball, or glove. In addition, the recorder receives two graphs: one will record predictions and the other will record actual occurrences.

For the first part of the experiment the leader rubs each person's balloon with the wool. Each student sees if the spoon will be attracted to their balloon and will move toward it. Will the spoon be attracted to the negatively charged side of the balloon? It is. Nothing occurs when another part of the balloon is held up to it.

Then it is time to experiment with different objects. The task is to rub a balloon with the object students have been given and then to see if the spoon will be drawn toward the balloon. The experiment will show if their comb, scarf, ball, or glove can make a surface of the balloon negatively charged so that the positively charged spoon will move back and forth as the balloon is moved toward and away from it.

First, students predict whether their object will move the spoon. The recorder writes each person's prediction on a chart (see Figure 5.14) and asks why they predicted as they did. After students have explained their predictions, the experiments begin and the recorder marks a second similar chart as to whether or not the object moved the spoon. Students hypothesize as to why their predictions were verified or refuted.

Kevin gives them four questions to guide the follow-up discussion:

Why did the spoon move with certain objects and not with others?

What was the difference between these objects?

What do you think made the balloon move?

How is this experiment related to George, who we met in the beginning of class?

The reporter prepares to share the results with the whole class. By the end of the experiment students are very excited and eager to try more objects.

Kevin tells the class, "Make a list of what objects you'd like to try rubbing against the balloon and have another column indicating whether you think the object will or won't attract the balloon." The group eagerly begins this new phase.

Figure 5.14
Chart for Experiment I

This object will move the spoon!				
This object will not move the spoon!				
OBJECTS:	COMB	SCARF	BALL	GLOVE

Experiment II

Meanwhile, another group is conducting a different experiment with four students assuming the same roles. The organizer dispenses a clear plastic cup, a square of plastic wrap, and a rubber band to each group member. The leader dispenses eight pieces of rice cereal to each. Students place the cereal in the cup, cover it with the plastic wrap, and secure it with a rubber band (see Figure 5.15). The students predict how many pieces of cereal they can get to stick to the top of the wrap when they rub it on an object such as the top of their heads.

The predictions for each group member are recorded on the Predictions Chart (see Figure 5.16, page 198).

Following the experiment the group discusses whether their predictions were verified or refuted and why their experiments turned out as they did. Kevin provides some questions for their discussion:

Why did the pieces stick to the plastic?

Did each of us do something different to cause different results?

What else might we rub the plastic against to make the cereal stick?

The recorder then leads the group in filling in what they discovered (see Figure 5.17, page 198) and prepares to share the results with the class.

Grammar Rap

Jeralyn and Kevin have studied the school's fifth-grade curriculum guide and know that comma usage is taught and reviewed periodically. They want to embed the grammar within the actual context of reading and writing material; therefore, they select a sentence from *What's the Big Idea, Ben Franklin?* and create a Grammar Rap worksheet for the students to practice placing commas (see Figure 5.18, page 199).

The reporter from each group presents the results. Then each group questions members of the other group. The lesson concludes with much enthusiasm about how electricity works and suggestions of other experiments to try.

Figure 5.15
Experiment II

Created by Kia Eisenga, Calvin College, and adapted from illustrations by Sheryl Merier (1991), *Glide Into Winter With Math and Science*.

Figure 5.16
Predictions Chart

How Many Pieces Will Stick?

Names:	- - -	- - -	- - -	- - -	- - -	- - -	- - -	- - -	- - -
Number:	0	1	2	3	4	5	6	7	8

Figure 5.17
What We Discovered

1.
2.
3.
4.
5.

Summary

Kevin and Jeralyn have succeeded in getting the students actively involved in a lesson while generating excitement for the study of electricity. They have used cooperative learning and structured each group by assigning roles. They have arranged for the students to engage in a great deal of thinking, through predicting, refuting or verifying, and

Figure 5.18
Grammar Rap

Let's Practice Grammar! ! !

Directions: This is a sentence from the story we read today. Your job is to put the commas into the correct places in the sentence.

Once before a large audience in Spain 180 grenadiers were linked together by wire then given a shock to make them jump into the air at the same time.

then hypothesizing as to why the results turned out as they did. They have extended thought by having students suggest possibilities beyond their particular experiments. Perhaps most important they have created momentum for the study of history and science and their current applications in their lives.

GEORGE WASHINGTON'S MOTHER

(by Jean Fritz, ill. by DyAnne DiSalvo–Ryan)

The life and times of Mary Ball Washington, her famous son George, and her other children are described in an easy flowing narrative with numerous well–drawn colored illustrations.

Children Choices for 1993. Reprinted from *The Reading Teacher*, October 1993.

 Activities for This Book

Building interest
Making predictions
Considering the historical period
Predicting and brainstorming
Predicting items' importance in story
Predicting characteristics of Mary Washington
Reading aloud by teachers

"Finger following" by students
Review and discussion
Checking predictions
Proving or disproving predictions
Modeling teacher read aloud
Writing a letter to mom or grandma
Poetry from the content area
Using prediction chart words
Writing a biopoem

Pennie Hale and Kris LeMahieu have a group of fifth graders who read at a lower level than the other three groups working with Jean Fritz books. Jean Fritz's books, however, connect to diverse reading abilities.

When Pennie and Kris enter the classroom to collect their students, Erin Mulhall, the fifth–grade teacher, calls out the names of seven students to read *George Washington's Mother*, just as she has assigned other groups to a book title. Pennie and Kris have tailored their lesson for

these students. The excerpt from the book that these students will read
is at an easier reading level than the books their peers are reading. Furthermore, Pennie and Kris are prepared to engage in a variety of sup-
portive oral reading activities to assist the students as needed. They will
also participate in exciting literature response activities because lower
readers should not be consigned to lower level tasks.

Building Interest

A box arrives in the room by messenger; it is addressed to King
George Washington.

Pennie asks, "I wonder what could be in the box?"

Saron answers, "A gun?"

"From whom did the box come? Check the return address," says
Pennie.

Lindsay responds, "From his mother. She wouldn't send a gun!"

"She'd send him food; that's what all mothers send," April chimes in.

"Good guess." Pennie urges, "What else might be in there?"

Johnnie exclaims, "I hope it is candy bars!"

"Do you think they had candy bars in George Washington's time?"
Pennie reasons.

Students continue to brainstorm and Pennie asks them to think of
the times in which George Washington's mother might have sent him
a package. She reminds them of what they had studied about the American Revolution.

Opening the Box

When she opens the box, Pennie reveals a letter, a butter wrapper,
tissues, flowers (dead and shriveled), and gingerbread. Before proceed-
ing with the lesson, Pennie leads the students in a discussion of the
items: why they might have been sent, how important they may have
been at that time, and whether they would be sent in a package to a
soldier today.

Predicting and Brainstorming

Kris takes over the lesson and introduces a prediction chart (see Figure 5.19).

She asks the students to predict what each of the items might mean in the story. She serves as scribe, recording the students' answers in the "I think…" column. Then she asks the students to predict the characteristics of Mary, George Washington's mother, in the column "Mary is…." She links the predictions back to the items that Mary sent in the package to George.

Reading, Review, and Discussion

Pennie and Kris take turns reading aloud excerpts of the book while the students follow along. For part of the reading, they ask the students to follow along with their fingers. As this occurs, Pennie and Kris note

Figure 5.19
Prediction Chart

George Washington's Mother
by Jean Fritz

Predictions

item	"I think…"	Story showed…
kleenex	Mary is sad because he went to war blows her nose a lot	She was sad about George going to war.
flowers	She wants him to smell good / Proof that he got the letter / reminder of how she smelled	planted and gardened a lot
butter	ran out while baking – needs more	EXACTLY RIGHT! ☺
gingerbread	It's what she always bakes—George's favorite / Might run out of food at the war / It was George's birthday	
Mary is…	worried kind / responsible helpful / missing Georg / loving / generous	wondering / worrying / complaining / hoping

who is able to keep up with their finger tracking and who struggles to do so. They hope to work with these students individually later.

Following the reading, students review their predictions and offer proof by referring back to events in the story. Kris records their proof under the column "Story showed...." The students cite proof for their predictions about what the items might mean in the story and for their predictions about Mary.

Reading and Writing

The box also reveals a letter that George Washington's mother had written him. Kris reads it aloud to the class (see Figure 5.20). Then Pennie reads it aloud and invites students to do the same. Kris and Pennie figure that by each reading the letter aloud, they can demonstrate and model oral reading. They also provide the students with some preread-

Figure 5.20
Letter From George Washington's Mother

April 19, 1775

Dear George,
    Why must you go to war? Don't you care about your poor mother? What will become of me? Come home right away and send money! Love Always, Mom

P.S. I have sent you some things from home.

ing preparation to enable them to feel capable reading the letter aloud to peers to practice oral fluency. Pennie and Kris then invite the students to write a letter that their mother or grandmother might write to them if they were away for a summer. What might their mother or grandmother say? What might they send in a package?

After sharing their letters with each other, the students are ready for another kind of writing.

Poetry From the Content Area

Pennie and Kris introduce the biopoem. They tell the students that there is a lot of information about George Washington's mother in the prediction chart on the wall from which they can obtain words. Students readily borrow from the chart as their biopoems develop. Lindsay's biopoem captures Mary's turmoil and her problems (see Figure 5.21).

Figure 5.21
Biopoem of Mary Washington

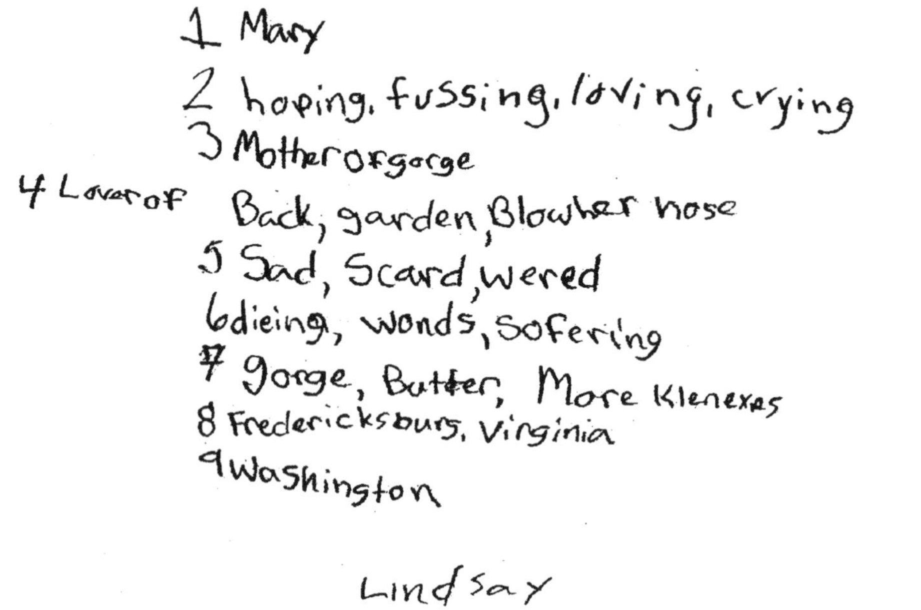

1 Mary
2 hoping, fussing, loving, crying
3 Mother of george
4 Lover of   Back, garden, Blow her nose
5 Sad, Scard, wered
6 dieing, wonds, sofering
7 gorge, Butter, More Klenexes
8 Fredericksburg, Virginia
9 Washington

Lindsay

Concluding With Mary's Gingerbread

The students have not forgotten that they will get to sample Mary Washington's gingerbread. Pennie reminds them that they have to decide if it is from Mary's time. If so, what would it be like? "Hard. Wormy," speculate the students. Pennie tells them that the end or crust was called "the kissing piece," which no one ate. None of the students want it. They eagerly grab pieces and bite into them. They soon discover that Mary could not have made it. It is too moist, soft, and delicious.

"Say," says Pennie, eager to seize upon a teachable moment, "I noticed that you bit into the gingerbread 'gingerly.' Let's put that on our list for Word Study and see if there is a connection between *gingerly* and *gingerbread*." The students' mouths are too full of gingerbread to do more than mumble their agreement.

Children's Books Cited

Can't you make them behave, King George? (1996). New York: Putnam.
George Washington's mother. (1992). New York: Putnam.
What's the big idea, Ben Franklin? (1976). New York: Putnam.
Will you sign here, John Hancock? (1976). New York: Putnam.

Other Books by Jean Fritz

Autobiography

China homecoming. (1985). New York: Putnam.
Homesick: My own story. (1984). New York: Dell.
Surprising myself. (1992). Katonah, NY: Richard C. Owen.

Historical Novels

Brady. (1988). New York: Puffin.
The cabin faced west. (1987). New York: Puffin.
Early thunder. (1987). New York: Puffin.
George Washington's breakfast. (1984). New York: Putnam.

Biographies for 2nd Grade and Up

And then what happened, Paul Revere? (1973). New York: Putnam.
Just a few words, Mr. Lincoln. (1993). New York: Price Stern Sloan.
Shh! We're writing the Constitution. (1997). New York: Putnam.

Where do you think you're going, Christopher Columbus? (1981). New York: Putnam.
Where was Patrick Henry on the 29th of May? (1975). New York: Putnam.
Who's that stepping on Plymouth Rock? (1975). New York: Putnam.
Why don't you get a horse, Sam Adams? (1974). New York: Putnam.
You want women to vote, Lizzie Stanton? (1995). New York: Putnam.

Biographies for Upper Grade Levels

Bully for you, Teddy Roosevelt. (1991). New York: Putnam.
The double life of Pocahontas. (1987). New York: Puffin.
The great little Madison. (1989). New York: Putnam.
Harriet Beecher Stowe and the Beecher preachers. (1994). New York: Putnam.
Make way for Sam Houston. (1986). New York: Putnam.
Stonewall. (1979). New York: Putnam.
Traitor: The case of Benedict Arnold. (1989). New York: Puffin.

Plant a Seed—Read!

I found an idea in the leaves
Of a book
Or was it a tree?
I know it was a living thing.
It filled me with such awe
That I saved it between the
Leaves
Of my own dear book—
Or was it a forest of grand
And bold ideas
Ripe for me to wander
Through?
I know it was a living thing.

© 1999 by Walter Dean Myers
From bookmark © 1999 The Children's Book Council, Inc.

These words of inspiration are printed on one of the bookmarks published each year by the Children's Book Council to inspire teachers and students to use children's and adolescent literature in the classroom. The theme of the poem, planting the idea of reading, expresses what teachers do in motivating students toward literacy. Through the innovative use of literature in the classroom, teachers can indeed plant a seed, nurture and nourish it, and see it come to full bloom. What challenge there is in the process and what excitement there is when a motivated reader is created. The blooming of a motivated reader connects with competency in listening, speaking, and writing and reaches beyond language arts into the content areas.

The teachers and classroom scenes we have described offer a variety of literacy—reading, writing, listening, speaking—activities centered around Children's Choices books. We have included a variety of genres and made content area connections. We have represented books that have appeared on the lists across the years since its inception in 1974, selecting books that remain popular in diverse classrooms: urban and suburban, private and public school, and in different areas of the United States. We offered books as they were used in classrooms from early elementary through middle school, and presented some unique uses of books, stretching the grade and reading levels from which they were originally categorized. Some of the titles and several of the activities make provisions for at-risk readers, those reading below grade level or lacking in literacy skills.

We salute the teachers and future teachers who shared their ideas with us. We challenge other teachers to use and expand on these ideas, applying their own ideas and interests, as well as their knowledge of their curriculum and their students' needs, to extend the activities and create their own literacy experiences from the thousands of Children's Choices books in publication. We agree with Routman (2000) who

> encourages teachers to choose books that engage students but that also, with guidance, can challenge their "view of the world" and trigger deeper understanding…that deal with broad themes, historical periods, or science as part of life; those written by notable authors; and those that are beautifully written…. The book must be a pleasure to read…. We want students to delight in literature so they will choose to go on reading. (p. 181)

We think that the books we have presented meet these criteria. Our hope is that teachers and students will be inspired to plant their own seeds of literacy and see the seeds flower and produce lifelong readers and writers.

REFERENCES

Allen, R.V. (1976). *Language experiences in communication*. Boston: Houghton Mifflin.

Allington, R.L., & Walmsley, S.A. (Eds.). (1995). *No quick fix: Rethinking literacy programs in America's elementary schools*. New York: Teachers College Press, and Newark, DE: International Reading Association.

Almasi, J.F. (1996). A new view of discussion. In L.B. Gambrell & J.F. Almasi (Eds.), *Lively discussions: Fostering engaged reading* (pp. 2–24). Newark, DE: International Reading Association.

Anderson, R.C., & Pearson, P.D. (1984). A schema-theoretic view of basic processes in reading comprehension. In P.D. Pearson (Ed.), *Handbook of reading research* (Vol. 1, pp. 255–291). New York: Longman.

Atwell, N. (1987). *In the middle: Writing, reading, and learning with adolescents*. Portsmouth, NH: Boynton/Cook.

Atwell, N. (1998). *In the middle: New understandings about reading, writing, and learning* (2nd ed.). Portsmouth, NH: Boynton/Cook.

Battle, J. (1995). Collaborative story talk in a bilingual kindergarten. In N.L. Roser & M.G. Martinez (Eds.), *Book talk and beyond: Children and teachers respond to literature* (pp. 157–167). Newark, DE: International Reading Association.

Beck, I.L. (1998). Understanding beginning reading: A journey through teaching and research. In J. Osborn & F. Lehr (Eds.), *Literacy for all: Issues in teaching and learning* (pp. 11–31). New York: Guilford Press.

Beyer, B.K. (1988). *Developing a thinking skills program*. Boston: Allyn & Bacon.

Bishop, R.S. (1992). Extending multicultural understanding. In B.E. Cullinan (Ed.), *Invitation to read: More children's literature in the reading program* (pp. 80–91). Newark, DE: International Reading Association.

Button, K., Johnson, M., & Furgerson, P. (1996). Interactive writing in a primary classroom. *The Reading Teacher, 49*, 446–454.

Campbell, R. (Ed.). (1998). *Facilitating preschool literacy*. Newark, DE: International Reading Association.

Carter, B., & Abrahamson, R.F. (1992). Factual history: Nonfiction in the social studies program. In B.E. Cullinan (Ed.), *Fact and fiction: Literature across the curriculum* (pp. 31–56). Newark, DE: International Reading Association.

Clay, M. (1975). *What did I write?* Auckland, NZ: Heinemann.

Cohn, D., & Wendt, S.J. (1992). Literature adds up for math class. In B.E. Cullinan (Ed.), *Fact and fiction: Literature across the curriculum* (pp. 57–67). Newark, DE: International Reading Association.

Collins, J.J. (1992). *Developing writing and thinking skills across the curriculum: A practical program for schools*. Rowley, MA: The Network.

Cramer, E.H. (1994). Connecting in the classroom: Ideas from teachers. In E.H. Cramer & M. Castle (Eds.), *Fostering the love of reading: The affective domain in reading education* (pp. 125–141). Newark, DE: International Reading Association.

Cramer, E.H., & Castle, M. (1994). Developing lifelong readers. In E.H. Cramer & M. Castle (Eds.), *Fostering the love of reading: The affective domain in reading education* (pp. 3–9). Newark, DE: International Reading Association.

Cullinan, B.E. (Ed.). (1987). *Children's literature in the reading program.* Newark, DE: International Reading Association.

Cullinan, B.E. (1992a). *Fact and fiction: Literature across the curriculum.* Newark, DE: International Reading Association.

Cullinan, B.E. (Ed.). (1992b). *Invitation to read: More children's literature in the reading program.* Newark, DE: International Reading Association.

Cullinan, B.E. (1995). In N.L. Roser & M.G. Martinez (Eds.), *Book talk and beyond: Children and teachers respond to literature* (p. ix). Newark, DE: International Reading Association.

Cullinan, B.E., Scala, M.C., & Schroder, V.C. (1995). *Three voices: An invitation to poetry across the curriculum.* York, ME: Stenhouse.

Cunningham, P.M., Hall, D.P., & Defee, M. (1991). Nonability grouped, multilevel instruction: A year in a first grade classroom. *The Reading Teacher, 44,* 566–571.

Cunningham, P.M., Hall, D.P., & Defee, M. (1998). Nonability-grouped, multilevel instruction: Eight years later. *The Reading Teacher, 51,* 652–664.

Eeds, M., & Peterson, R.L. (1995). What teachers need to know about the literary craft. In N.L. Roser & M.G. Martinez (Eds.), *Book talk and beyond: Children and teachers respond to literature* (pp. 10–23). Newark, DE: International Reading Association.

Farris, P.J. (1997). *Language arts: Process, product, and assessment* (2nd ed.). New York: McGraw-Hill.

Flippo, R.F. (1999). *What do the experts say? Helping children learn to read.* Portsmouth, NH: Heinemann.

Freeman, E.B., & Person, D.G. (Eds.). (1992). *Using nonfiction trade books in the elementary classroom: From ants to zeppelins.* Urbana, IL: National Council of Teachers of English.

Gaines, P.G. (1992). Invite children to respond using the fine arts. In E.B. Freeman & D.G. Person (Eds.), *Using nonfiction trade books in the elementary classroom: From ants to zeppelins* (pp. 95–103). Urbana, IL: National Council of Teachers of English.

Gambrell, L.B., & Almasi, J.F. (Eds.). (1996). *Lively discussions: Fostering engaged reading.* Newark, DE: International Reading Association.

Gardner, H. (1983). *Frames of mind: The theory of multiple intelligences.* New York: Basic.

Gardner, H., & Hatch, T. (1989). Multiple intelligences go to school. *Educational Researcher, 18*(8), 4–10.

Glazer, S.M., & Burke, E.M. (1994). *An integrated approach to early literacy: Literature to language.* Boston: Allyn & Bacon.

Goodman, K.S. (1986). *What's whole in whole language?* Portsmouth, NH: Heinemann.

Goodman, K.S. (1992). Whole language research: Foundations and development. In S.J. Samuels & A.E. Farstrup (Eds.), *What research has to say about reading instruction*

(2nd ed., pp. 46–69). Newark, DE: International Reading Association. (Originally published in *Elementary Journal, 90*(2), 1989.)

Goodman, K.S. (1996). *On reading*. Portsmouth, NH: Heinemann.

Graves, D. (1983). *Writing: Teachers and children at work*. Portsmouth, NH: Heinemann.

Graves, D. (1994). *A fresh look at writing*. Portsmouth, NH: Heinemann.

Greenlaw, M.J., & McIntosh, M.E. (1987). Science fiction and fantasy worth teaching to teens. In B.E. Cullinan (Ed.), *Invitation to read: More children's literature in the reading program* (pp. 111-120). Newark, DE: International Reading Association.

Gunning, T.G. (1998). *Best books for beginning readers*. Boston: Allyn & Bacon.

Guthrie, J.T., & Wigfield, A. (1997). Reading engagement: A rationale for theory and teaching. In J.T. Guthrie & A. Wigfield (Eds.), *Reading engagement: Motivating readers through integrated instruction* (pp. 1–12). Newark, DE: International Reading Association.

Hall, D.P., Prevatte, C., & Cunningham, P. (1995). Eliminating ability grouping and reducing failure in the primary grades. In R.L. Allington & S.A. Walmsley (Eds.), *No quick fix: Rethinking literacy programs in America's elementary schools* (pp. 137–158). New York: Teachers College Press; Newark, DE: International Reading Association.

Harris, T.L., & Hodges, R.E. (Eds.). (1995). *The literacy dictionary: The vocabulary of reading and writing*. Newark, DE: International Reading Association.

Hennings, D.G. (1997). *Communication in action: Teaching the language arts*. Boston: Houghton Mifflin.

Henning, D.G. (200). *Communication in action: Teaching literature-based language arts*. Boston: Houghton Mifflin.

Holdaway, D. (1979). The foundations of literacy. Portsmouth, NH: Heinemann.

Huck, C.S., & Kerstetter, K.J. (1987). Developing readers. In B.E. Cullinan (Ed.), *Children's literature in the reading program* (pp. 30–40). Newark, DE: International Reading Association.

Hynds, S. (1997). *On the brink: Negotiating literature and life with adolescents*. New York: Teachers College Press; Newark, DE: International Reading Association.

International Reading Association. (1996). *More teachers' favorite books for kids: Teachers' choices 1994–1996*. Newark, DE: Author.

Kiefer, B.Z. (1995). Responding to literature as art in picture books. In N.L. Roser & M.G. Martinez (Eds.), *Book talk and beyond: Children and teachers respond to literature* (pp. 191–200). Newark, DE: International Reading Association.

Kneedler, P. (1985). California assesses critical thinking. In A. Costa (Ed.), *Developing minds: A resource book for teaching thinking* (pp. 276–280). Alexandria, VA: Association for Supervision and Curriculum Development.

Langer, J.A. (1995). *Envisioning literature: Literary understanding and literature instruction*. New York: Teachers College Press; Newark, DE: International Reading Association.

Lapp, D., & Flood, J. (1992). Literature in the science program. In B.E. Cullinan (Ed.), *Fact and fiction: Literature across the curriculum* (pp. 68–79). Newark, DE: International Reading Association.

Martinez, M.G., & Roser, N.L. (1995). The books make a difference in story talk. In N.L. Roser, & M.G. Martinez, (Eds.), *Book talk and beyond: Children and teachers respond to literature* (pp. 32–41). Newark, DE: International Reading Association.

Merier, S. (1991). *Glide into winter with math and science.* Fresno, CA: AIMS Educational Foundation.

McClure, A.A., & Kristo, J.V. (Eds.). (1994). *Inviting children's responses to literature: Guides to 57 notable books.* Urbana. IL: National Council of Teachers of English.

McGee, L.M. (1998). How do we teach literature to young children? In S.B. Neuman & K.A. Roskos (Eds.), *Children achieving: Best practices in early literacy* (pp. 162–179). Newark, DE: International Reading Association.

McMahon, S.I., & Raphael, T.E. (Eds.). (1997). *The book club connection: Literacy learning and classroom talk.* New York: Teachers College Press; Newark, DE: International Reading Association.

Michigan Reading Association. (1986). *New directions in reading.* Grand Rapids, MI: Author.

Monson, D. (1987). Characterization in literature: Realistic and historical fiction. In B.E. Cullinan (Ed.), *Children's literature in the reading program* (pp. 98–110). Newark, DE: International Reading Association.

Neuman, S.B., & Roskos, K.A. (1998). *Children achieving: Best practices in early literacy.* Newark, DE: International Reading Association.

Nurss, J.R., & Hough, R.A. (1992). Reading and the ESL student. In S.J. Samuels & A.E. Farstrup (Eds.), *What research has to say about reading instruction* (2nd ed., pp. 277–313). Newark, DE: International Reading Association.

Ogle, D.M. (1986). K-W-L: A teaching model that develops active reading of expository text. *The Reading Teacher, 39,* 564–570.

Pike, K., Compain, R., & Mumper, J. (1997). *New connections: An integrated approach to literacy.* New York: Addison-Wesley Longman.

Pressley, M. (1998). *Reading instruction that works: The case for balanced literacy.* New York: Guilford Press.

Raphael, T. (1986). Teaching Question-Answer Relationships, revisited. *The Reading Teacher, 39,* 516–622.

Richardson, J.S. (2000). *Read it aloud!: Using literature in the secondary content classroom.* Newark, DE: International Reading Association.

Rosenblatt, L.M. (1985). The transactional theory of the literary work: Implications for research. In C.F. Cooper (Ed.), *Researching response to literature and the teaching of literature* (pp. 33–53). Norwood, NJ: Ablex.

Roser, N.L., & Martinez, M.G. (Eds.). (1995). *Book talk and beyond: Children and teachers respond to literature.* Newark, DE: International Reading Association.

Routman, R. (1988). *Transitions: From literature to literacy.* Portsmouth, NH: Heinemann.

Routman, R. (1991). *Invitations.* Portsmouth, NH: Heinemann.

Routman, R. (2000). *Conversations: Strategies for teaching, learning, and evaluating.* Portsmouth, NH: Heinemann.

Rumelhart, D.E. (1980). Schemata: The building blocks of cognition. In R.J. Spiro, B.C. Bruce, & W.F. Brewer (Eds.), *Theoretical issues in reading comprehension* (pp. 33–58). Hillsdale, NJ: Erlbaum.

Samuels, S.J., Schermer, M., & Reinking, D. (1992). Reading fluency: Techniques for making decoding automatic. In S.J. Samuels & A.E. Farstrup (Eds.), *What research has to say about reading instruction* (2nd ed., pp. 124–144). Newark, DE: International Reading Association.

Schaffer, F. (1986–1987, November/December). Bounces, whoppers, and taradiddles. Terrific Tall Tales reproducible sheet. *Classmate*. Torrance, CA: Frank Schaffer Publications.

Schmidt, P.R. (1999). KWLQ: Inquiry and literacy learning in science. *The Reading Teacher, 52 ,* 789–792.

Sebesta, S.E. (1987). Enriching the arts and humanities through children's books. In B.E. Cullinan (Ed.), *Children's literature in the reading program* (pp. 50–63). Newark, DE: International Reading Association.

Sebesta, S.E. (1992). Enriching the arts and humanities. In B.E. Cullinan (Ed.), *Invitation to read: More children's literature in the reading program* (pp. 77–88). Newark, DE: International Reading Association.

Sinatra, R. (1994). Literature and the visual arts: Natural motivations for literacy. In E.H. Cramer & M. Castle (Eds.), *Fostering the love of reading: The affective domain in reading education* (pp. 104–117). Newark, DE: International Reading Association.

Slaughter, J.P. (1993). *Beyond storybooks: Young children and the shared book experience.* Newark, DE: International Reading Association.

Slavin, R.E. (1995). *Cooperative learning* (2nd ed.) Boston: Allyn & Bacon.

Smith, R.J., & Johnson, D.D. (1980). *Teaching children to read.* Reading, MA: Addison-Wesley.

Spiegel, D.L. (1992). Blending whole language and systematic direct instruction. *The Reading Teacher, 46,* 38–44.

Stauffer, R.G. (1970). *The language experience approach to the teaching of reading.* New York: HarperCollins.

Stauffer, R.G. (1975). *Directing the reading-thinking process.* New York: Harper & Row.

Stein, N.L., & Glenn, C.G. (1979). An analysis of story comprehension in elementary school children. In R.O. Freedle (Ed.), *New directions in discourse processing* (Vol. 2, pp. 53–120). Hillsdale, NJ: Ablex.

Stein, N.L., & Glenn, C.G. (1982). Children's concept of time: The development of a story schema. In W.J. Freidman (Ed.), *The developmental psychology of time* (pp. 255–282). New York: Academic Press.

Strickland, D.S. (1987). Children's literature: Key element in the language and reading program. In B.E. Cullinan (Ed.). *Children's literature in the reading program* (pp. 68–76). Newark, DE: International Reading Association.

Strickland, D.S., & Morrow, L.M. (Eds.). (1989). *Emerging literacy: Young children learn to read and write.* Newark, DE: International Reading Association.

Taylor, B., Short, R., Shearer, B., & Frye, B. (1995). First grade teachers provide early reading intervention in the classroom. In R.L. Allington & S.A. Walmsley (Eds.), *No quick fix: Rethinking literacy programs in America's elementary schools* (pp. 159–176). New York: Teachers College Press; Newark, DE: International Reading Association.

Teacher Created Materials. (1993). *Bear essentials: A newspaper of creative ideas for K-5 teachers, 1*(1). Westminster, CA: Author.

Trelease, J. (1989). *The new read aloud handbook* (2nd ed.). London: Penguin.

Trelease, J. (1995). *The read aloud handbook* (4th ed.). New York: Penguin.

Vacca, J.A., Vacca, R.T., & Gove, M.K. (1995). *Reading and learning to read* (3rd ed.). New York: Addison-Wesley.

Vacca, J.A., Vacca, R.T., & Gove, M.K. (2000). *Reading and learning to read* (4th ed.). New York: Addison-Wesley.

Vygotsky, L.S. (1978). *Mind in society: The development of higher psychological processes* (M. Cole, V. John-Steiner, S. Scribner, & E. Souberman, Eds. & Trans.). Cambridge, MA: Harvard University Press. (Original work published 1934)

Walp, T.P., & Walmsley, S.A. (1995). Scoring well on tests or becoming genuinely literate: Rethinking remediation in a small rural school. In R.L. Allington & S.A. Walmsley (Eds.), *No quick fix: Rethinking literacy programs in America's elementary schools* (pp. 177–196). New York: Teachers College Press; Newark, DE: International Reading Association.

Wigfield, A. (1997). Children's motivations for reading and reading engagement. In J.T. Guthrie & A. Wigfield (Eds.), *Reading engagement: Motivating readers through integrated instruction* (pp. 14–33). Newark, DE: International Reading Association.

Worthy, M.J., & Bloodgood, J.W. (1992/1993). Enhancing reading instruction through Cinderella tales. *The Reading Teacher, 46*, 260–301.

Children's Choices

International Reading Association. (1983). *Children's Choices: Teaching with books children like.* Newark, DE: Author.

Classroom Choices: Children's Trade Books 1974. Reproduced from November 1975 issue of *The Reading Teacher, 29*, Newark, DE: International Reading Association.

Classroom Choices: Children's Trade Books 1975. Reproduced from October 1976 issue of *The Reading Teacher, 30*, Newark, DE: International Reading Association.

Classroom Choices: Children's Trade Books 1977. Reproduced from October 1977 issue of *The Reading Teacher, 31*, Newark, DE: International Reading Association.

Classroom Choices: Children's Trade Books 1978. Reproduced from October 1978 issue of *The Reading Teacher, 32*, Newark, DE: International Reading Association.

Children's Choices for 1979. Reprinted from October 1979 issue of *The Reading Teacher, 33*, Newark, DE: International Reading Association.

Children's Choices for 1980. Reprinted from October 1980 issue of *The Reading Teacher, 34*, Newark, DE: International Reading Association.

Children's Choices for 1981. Reprinted from October 1981 issue of *The Reading Teacher, 35*, Newark, DE: International Reading Association.

Children's Choices for 1982. Reprinted from October 1982 issue of *The Reading Teacher, 36*, Newark, DE: International Reading Association.

Children's Choices for 1983. Reprinted from October 1983 issue of *The Reading Teacher, 37*, Newark, DE: International Reading Association.

Children's Choices for 1984. Reprinted from October 1984 issue of *The Reading Teacher*, *38*, Newark, DE: International Reading Association.

Children's Choices for 1985. Reprinted from October 1985 issue of *The Reading Teacher*, *39*, Newark, DE: International Reading Association.

Children's Choices for 1986. Reprinted from October 1986 issue of *The Reading Teacher*, *40*, Newark, DE: International Reading Association.

Children's Choices for 1987. Reprinted from October 1987 issue of *The Reading Teacher*, *41*, Newark, DE: International Reading Association.

Children's Choices for 1988. Reprinted from October 1988 issue of *The Reading Teacher*, *42*, Newark, DE: International Reading Association.

Children's Choices for 1989. Reprinted from October 1989 issue of *The Reading Teacher*, *43*, Newark, DE: International Reading Association.

Children's Choices for 1990. Reprinted from October 1990 issue of *The Reading Teacher*, *44*, Newark, DE: International Reading Association.

Children's Choices for 1991. Reprinted from October 1991 issue of *The Reading Teacher*, *45*, Newark, DE: International Reading Association.

Children's Choices for 1992. Reprinted from October 1992 issue of *The Reading Teacher*, *46*, Newark, DE: International Reading Association.

Children's Choices for 1993. Reprinted from October 1993 issue of *The Reading Teacher*, *47*, Newark, DE: International Reading Association.

Children's Choices for 1994. Reprinted from October 1994 issue of *The Reading Teacher*, *48*, Newark, DE: International Reading Association.

Children's Choices for 1995. Reprinted from October 1995 issue of *The Reading Teacher*, *49*, Newark, DE: International Reading Association.

Children's Choices for 1996. Reprinted from October 1996 issue of *The Reading Teacher*, *50*, Newark, DE: International Reading Association.

Children's Choices for 1997. Reprinted from October 1997 issue of *The Reading Teacher*, *51*, Newark, DE: International Reading Association.

Children's Choices for 1998. Reprinted from October 1998 issue of *The Reading Teacher*, *52*, Newark, DE: International Reading Association.

Children's Choices for 1999. Reprinted from October 1999 issue of *The Reading Teacher*, *53*, Newark, DE: International Reading Association.

INDEX

Page numbers followed by *f* indicate figures.

T–U

Printed in Canada